Tea and Talk

Praise for Alice Taylor's other books

Alice Taylor

I enjoy village living. Back in the early sixties when I came to live in Innishannon as a twenty-year-old newly-wed it was a very quiet place, traffic-free and tranquil. Uncle Jacky and Aunty Peg lived next door to us, and everyone living in the village knew one another.

A stranger was a great novelty. Now the population has exploded and the road through the village is throbbing with non-stop traffic. Over the years I have been part of the changing fabric of the village, and, while some changes have depleted us, others have enriched us. But the essence of our village life today remains intact due mainly to the solid core of farming life surrounding us and the generous people who give time and effort voluntarily to keep the heart of our community vibrant. Being part of a village community can be challenging and frustrating, but it is always interesting and enriching. I often walk the woods, watch the river, but above all share time with family, friends and neighbours. I am glad that I live here.

RECENT BOOKS BY ALICE TAYLOR
And Time Stood Still
The Gift of a Garden
Do You Remember?
The Women

For a complete list see www.obrien.ie

Tea and Talk

Alice Taylor

Photographs by Emma Byrne

Alia Taylor

BRANDON

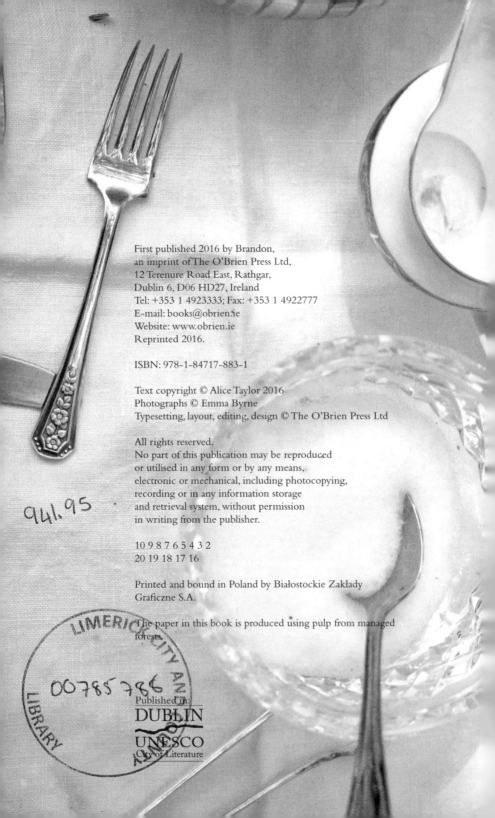

First published 2016 by Brandon,
an imprint of The O'Brien Press Ltd,
12 Terenure Road East, Rathgar,
Dublin 6, D06 HD27, Ireland
Tel: +353 1 4923333; Fax: +353 1 4922777
E-mail: books@obrien.ie
Website: www.obrien.ie
Reprinted 2016.

ISBN: 978-1-84717-883-1

10 9 8 7 6 5 4 3 2
20 19 18 17 16

Printed and bound in Poland by Białostockie Zakłady
Graficzne S.A.

The paper in this book is produced using pulp from managed
forests.

Published in:
DUBLIN
UNESCO
City of Literature

Dedication

For Gabriel, in grateful appreciation for the love of this place
that you nurtured in me.
And for Tim Gabriel, the newest arrival in our village.

Contents

Introduction

Under the Apple Tree

It is a beautiful day, and the garden is snoozing in the warm afternoon sun. A blackbird scratching under a nearby fern keeps a wary eye on the neighbour's cat who has just wandered in. But this cat is too old and too well fed to bother with a disturbing encounter. So the blackbird, absorbing the surrounding lethargy, fluffs out its wings and sits on the warm grass and sunbathes. The garden is a pool of relaxation and peace. You are welcome to join me here in my garden, my home, my own village.

Come out the back door. Take time to meander around the backyard, which has no illusions of grandeur. It is peopled by an assortment of ancient collectables called out of retirement to act as containers for impulsively purchased garden-centre enticements. The result is a riot of unimaginable colour and confusion, which leads you to the conclusion that the gardener here is either a genius or a green-fingered eccentric, but probably the latter.

Your eye is caught by a rose-smothered arch, which suggests that beyond this could be the real garden. Arches in gardens are an invitation into another section. Having come through this arch you are hoping to find a decision point, but more arched pathways lead left, right and straight ahead. A trifle confusing. You wish that the gardener here could make up her mind as to what direction you are meant to go. You feel sure that it is a woman! No man would garden like this – men think in straight lines, don't they? So you go straight ahead towards a stone, weather-beaten St Joseph holding a lily in his raised hand. But the lily is broken, leaving Joseph with half a lily. Typical! Then another rose-covered arch leads off to your left, so you take it and arrive under an ancient apple tree, where a rug-covered garden seat invites you to take a rest. This is Uncle Jacky's apple tree. You sit down and relax. Belying its antiquity, the seat is surprisingly comfortable. This is heaven. Just sit there quietly now and enjoy the experience. Soon I will bring you tea in the garden.

I dress the tray carefully with china cups and Aunty Peg's silver teapot. After all, this tea in the garden is not just a casual affair, it is a ceremonial event of elegance and decorum. Because, in the course of this tea, we are going to exchange good conversation, and I will tell you interesting stories about this place where I live.

Over fifty years ago I came to this village of Innishannon. I was young and foolish, but the village was old and wise, and over the years this ancient place and its people have taught me many things. I was lucky to have married into a family who loved this place and had lived here for several generations. From them I learnt the old names of the townlands around the village, Gaelic names that run off the tongue like onomatopoeic poetry – Clouracaun, Dernagasha, Rathnaroughy – their murmuring sounds a meandering stream against mossy banks.

The placenames around the village tell the story of its roots. There is a little lane at the eastern end of the village known as Bothairín an Átha, which, translated, means 'the little road to the ford'. In ancient times, waterways were the arteries of the country, and while roads were still dirt tracks and before bridges were built, river crossings were of huge commercial importance. The Bandon river is tidal up to our village, and when the tide withdraws down to Kinsale harbour where the river enters the sea, it is fordable. The village grew up around this river crossing, which was the first point of access for the rest of the country into West Cork.

Time inevitably brings change, but the retention of the old placenames incorporates the past history of Innishannon into the present. It makes this village a historic and

interesting place to live. It is probably one of the reasons why this garden breathes of another era.

I was a blow-in, of course, but loved the village from the first day that I came here and the village opened its arms to me. That was over fifty years ago. Let me tell you of my life here now in this house and in this village.

But first, would you like another cup of tea?

Chapter 1

The Corner House

This morning, having had a leisurely breakfast, I picked up the daily paper for a general perusal. Never a good idea if you wish to maintain a sunny outlook on life. International upheavals screamed from the headlines, competing with home-grown conflicts. All of which could convince one that we are living in a crazy world. Then a news item caught my eye: 'Older people to be encouraged to downsize in order to ease the housing crisis.' *What a good idea*, I thought. Then, like chain lightning, came the realisation that they were talking about ME. Now, that was a horse of a different colour! The thought of leaving my own comfortable corner had never entered my mind.

The original name of this old house was the Corner House, which very aptly describes it, as it is plonk bang on the village corner. It feels like part of the village and of the community all around it. This house would give Dermot Bannon, of the TV programme *Room to Improve*, a heart attack as it defies all the rules of good house design. Also, most callers find their way in through the side door, never the front door, a practice Dermot declares to be a totally weird Irish phenomenon. In my case, though, there is worse to come, as this side door leads not into a well-laid-out hallway designed to impress, but into a utilitarian storeroom full of uninspiring clutter, with three steps leading down into the kitchen. Not exactly the scenario for good first impressions. However, my friends have been using this route for so long they never even see the state of it. At least, so I hope!

If a knock comes to the front door I sometimes may not even hear as it is so far away from the kitchen, and when I do hear one I immediately straighten myself up and wonder what they might be looking for. This is probably a hangover from my childhood when nobody except a policeman or a drainage inspector knocked on the door at all. Everyone else just walked in. One grand old man always came with the salutation, 'Peace be to this house.' What a lovely blessing he brought with him. I now have one friend who, when she comes in, simply calls out, 'It's me.'

If I go out to the garden, I have an antique wooden sign informing callers 'I'm in the Garden' which I leave on the centre of the kitchen table. This was given to me by an irritated friend who on a few occasions, having searched the whole house, finally ran me down outside. That sign now directs callers out the back door (not the side door, which opens onto the street) and into the garden, as that is usually where I am to be found if the weather is kind.

This house once creaked at the seams with people, as it began its life as a guest house. It then adapted itself as a rambling family home, and now I am home alone. Yet I never feel alone here. This is a comforting place to be, and in a strange way this old house has changed with the varying needs of the times and has somehow stretched and shrunk to meet requirements. I have never felt that it was too big or too small, always just right for the times that were in it. It is perfect for holding fund-raising coffee mornings or impromptu meetings, and because of its location it is very easy for newcomers to find. It's a wonderful base for family gatherings such as christenings, funerals, or during weddings for that awkward stopover period between church and reception — and if certain family members need distance from each other this can easily be achieved.

It is also an Aladdin's cave of all kinds of everything, things that are invaluable if we in the village are hosting a folk day, a church concert or anything requiring candles, containers

or decorations of any kind. If I lived in a tidy bungalow I simply could not harbour all these wacky requirements. There is a cupboard full of candles of all dimensions and varying colours: these are the result of candlelit church concerts and a once-off candle-making enterprise to aid a village fund-raiser. To assist in that enterprise the butts of years of leftover church candles found their way to our temporary factory. Earlier this year when an American friend celebrating Thanksgiving experienced a power failure, this stock of candles quickly solved his lighting problem. So the candles remain, and the room holding them smells like Rathborne's.

Then, accompanying them are the oil lamps. Maybe because I was reared in the glow of these I am fascinated by them and have collected some over the years. They are mostly elegant and useless, but lovely to look at. I bought the first one when we purchased this house as it was in the auction of contents and I simply could not resist it, even though at the time we were jumping to the shrieks of an irate bank manager. It cost the princely sum of eleven shillings which in today's money is a tiny amount. It has required occasional polishing to keep a smile on its face but, strangely enough, I like doing that because polishing old brass and silver can be quite soothing. And, as it is not good for one lamp to be alone over the years, it has acquired a number of lighting companions that have

never shed light on anything because candles come to the rescue much more quickly when there is a power failure. The lamps, however, are perched around the house like the decorative ladies of earlier times, giving the look but not the light of other days.

Chapter 2

Aunty Peg's Press

It had been bugging me for years. Every time I opened it to take out a tablecloth, place mat, oven glove or cloth of any description, I recoiled in dismay at the chaos within. To quote my father: 'There was not head, arse nor tail to it.' He was not into genteel statements of understated delicacy but graphic pronouncements that hit the nail dead on the head.

When Aunty Peg passed away in the late seventies, her press was passed on to me. Previously it had resided in one of her little parlours and had been maintained in exemplary condition. Strange as it may seem, she had three tiny parlours which, if all were rolled into one, would still have been a small room, but the three separate rooms evolved because with each addition to the back of their house when another

little room was added, the walls were considered too wide to be movable and were simply left in place. The result was that the middle parlour had no window, and this large oak press occupied most of the space. It was originally described as a 'press bed', and how it evolved from being a bed to just a press I have no idea.

Here Aunty Peg kept all her tablecloths, curtains and bedlinen, and because she was fond of such things she had accumulated a sizeable collection over the years. It was long before drip-dry and non-iron fabrics, so much of her time was given to washing, bleaching, starching and ironing. I loved her linen press. It always smelt of carbolic soap, Robin starch and lavender from the garden. After her death, the press moved across the garden into my storeroom off the kitchen. Into it went all her beautiful cloths plus my own accumulation, all arranged in pristine order.

The contents of the press grew and grew over the years because I am an antique-fair addict. And when I visit an antique fair I make straight for the linen table and drool over the hand-embroidered cloths, visualising robed sisters in convent gardens and elegant ladies of leisure in great houses gracefully engaged. These skilled needlewomen created beautiful heirlooms. All such ladies are long gone but have left behind them drawers full of delicate needlework now finding their way into the hands of the hurried masses coming after them. Such acquisitions deserve impeccable care. Hence the guilt when viewing the chaos of Aunty Peg's press in recent times. I could no longer bear it; Shakespeare was wise when he told us that conscience makes cowards of us all. The day of reckoning had come. Today I would tackle the press.

As soon as I opened my eyes this morning I informed my brain that today was the day for the press, and as soon as I came downstairs into the kitchen I went up the three steps that lead into the storeroom, a relic from my catering days. I opened the double doors of the press as far back as they would go and steeled myself to view the three deep shelves of disorder facing me. All this was about to change, change utterly, because order and beauty were about to be restored.

I left the door down into the kitchen open so that the press was in my face during breakfast. This was to combat any last-minute change of mind. Having eaten, I cleared the table and the dresser tops and pulled back all the chairs from the table. A casual caller could have thought that an operation was about to take place or that I was about to kill a pig! Beginning with the top shelf, I lifted out armfuls of cloths and dumped them down on the kitchen table until it was submerged. This particular table is no miniature, having been made big and ample by cousin Con when its forerunner collapsed. He was no mean carpenter, and he made it inside in the kitchen, and if it ever has to be evicted it will first need to be dismantled. During my tenure it will remain where it is as it is ideal for hosting family gatherings, sorting papers or

conducting impromptu meetings. A table brings immediate law and order to a meeting, I believe. Now it would hopefully bring the same to my unruly press.

By the time the press was empty, the table had disappeared beneath a deluge of cloth, every chair was occupied and the dresser tops were laden. I had made a resolution not to sort anything before or during transit but to land everything and then begin. I allocated a chair for oven gloves, a chair for tea cosies, a chair for aprons, a chair for table runners, a chair for place mats, a chair for serviettes. Then I ran out of chairs. The phone rang. An intermission.

I soon had to create space on the dresser tops to carry the overflow of place mats. *How many sets of place mats does one need?* I asked myself. I had no idea that I had so many. They had accumulated over the years and got buried. Tea towels too good for everyday use but with scenes that I 'might one day get around to painting' rolled out before me. They were lovely, but I vowed that I was never again going to visit a kitchen design shop. There were oven gloves, some of them well past their safety date. And there were scorched tea cosies, kept and treasured because I loved the knitter. I had definitely reached a place called 'Stop'.

With all the chair contents sorted, it was time to tackle the table. Now, where to start? At the very beginning, as Julie Andrews advised, was a very good place to start. So the first tablecloth that ever came my way was burrowed out to lay the foundation for the restoration. It brought back memories. During my first year of marriage, two long-lost American cousins came to visit Aunty Peg, and she decided that this saucy young new arrival living next door, who was married to her nephew and thought she knew everything, could do the entertaining. So she moved them in with me. I thought they were ancient, but they were years younger than I am now – age is relative! We got on fine, and when they went back to America they sent me an enormous banqueting tablecloth with matching napkins. I was very impressed, and during my early years of domesticity this cloth graced christening tables, First Holy Communion tables and birthday tables. A good-quality tablecloth makes a statement. When the big parlour table on the home farm where I grew up was draped with a white linen tablecloth, it immediately proclaimed celebration and entertainment. It heralded a big event. To this day, I am a sucker for a quality tablecloth and serviettes. But sorting out Aunty Peg's press now made me realise that I had gone way past the bounds of normality in this sphere.

The door opened, and a neighbour's head appeared. 'Are you having a jumble sale?' he wanted to know. 'Do you want to help?' I asked, and he disappeared.

Cloth stacks of different sizes began to grow around the table like high-rise tower blocks. I dug out matching serviettes from the general clutter. Long gone are the days

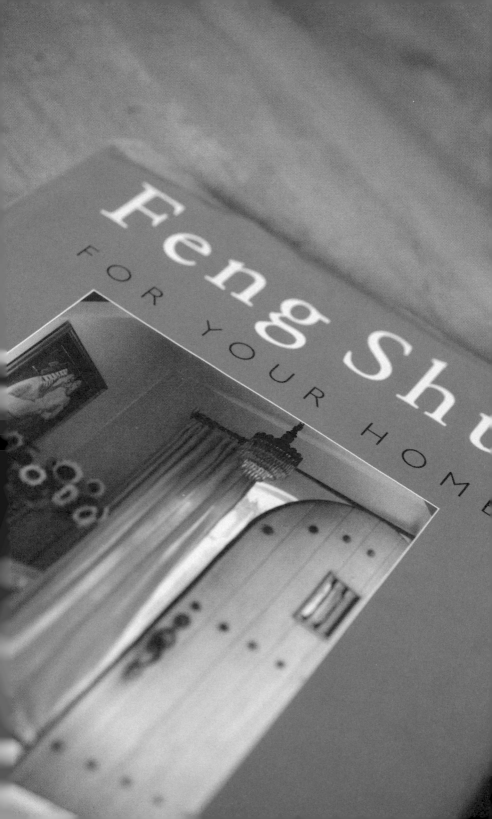

of matching serviettes, but I had inherited them, and they deserved respect. Then I had bought another special Christmas set with my sister in Toronto, and they had the names of all Santa's reindeers embroidered on them. Though used every Christmas, some spares still remained in pristine condition in their original beautiful box, but when I tried to put the laundered ones back into the box, I failed. Then I remembered the instructions of Sr Ita, who, many moons ago, taught us the art of good laundering in Drishane convent: a linen serviette, she had shown us, should be folded in three before ironing. I now did exactly that, and they slid perfectly back into their box. Good old Sr Ita! When I checked the names in the box, I discovered that Rudolf was missing, and I remembered that he had been absent for the previous Christmas dinner as well. I rooted and searched, but Rudolf was nowhere to be found. He must have strayed up into the hot press. I would unearth him and have him back on the team for next Christmas. The phone rang again, and a long conversation ensued. I was glad of the break.

Then back to business. Hard to believe that I am a regular reader of books on feng shui, which is the art of decluttering. One of the little gems that I've learnt is the necessity to have a container on hand when sorting: you need a deposit box for things that must not return from whence they came. So, to be sure to be sure, I placed a large box beside the table. Into this would go contributions for the hospice, which has a collection point at the end of the village. I tried to apply the 'when in doubt throw it out' strategy rather than the 'that could come in handy someday' philosophy. At the end of the sorting, the hospice box was almost full, but I still had a miscellaneous collection of no-fixed-abode articles. This is the rock on which you could wither when decluttering, so before the Scrooge in me surfaced, I caught them all and landed them into the box.

Then began the big return. The press was cleaned out, polished and lined with special lavender-scented drawer liners. There was a lot of depositing and withdrawing while I worked out the best location strategy: the Christmas section, the garden section, the posh-use section, the non-iron section. Then the place mats, greatly reduced, and the thinned-out tea cosies. As the press began to fill up, it took on the look of a nun's cupboard. I felt my halo settle firmly over my head.

Tidying a press is good for mind and body. The feng shui experts tell us: tidy your house, tidy your mind. Begin with just one drawer and make a good job of it. The rest will follow on. My mother had the philosophy that if you were having a bad day or if the day was wet and dismal you should tidy a press for therapy. She had never heard of feng shui, but, wise woman that she was, she had figured it out for herself.

Another plus to press tidying, which you will not find in any feng shui book, is that it is a wonderful colonic cleanser.

All the bending and stooping is great for irrigation purposes! When the press is done, you finish up with a clean mind, a clean colon, plus the clean press! As I viewed my tidied press, wallowing in a glow of self-satisfaction, I determined that it would never again slide back into its former state of confusion. But it probably will …

Chapter 3

Goodbye, Kate and Lolly

The day we buried Kate was an overcast, miserable day. The sky lay like a sodden grey sheet over Innishannon. Paddy, my good friend and neighbour, already had the grave dug when I climbed up the stone steps into his hilltop garden. All was shrouded in a clinging mist, and raindrops slithered off the overhanging trees onto the freshly dug brown mound of heaped earth. The grave was deep, short and solid and in an odd way strangely comforting. This was to be Kate's last resting place. Going down into the red earth of Farnagow overlooking the village would be her final journey.

We went across the yard to the grain barn where we had laid Kate's body the previous night on coming home from the vet. When we opened the door, the rich smell of newly milled grain encompassed us. Paddy carried her across the yard and up the steps in the tartan blanket that Gavin, the vet, had wrapped her in the previous night. Over my arm I had a big old Kerry Woollen Mills blanket belonging to Aunty Peg, who in her day had loved dogs.

We transferred Kate into the Kerry blanket and wrapped her up firmly. She seemed to have grown in death, and her long limbs, that in life were fluid and flexible, now extended rigidly. We eased them in against her body and wrapped the blanket around her. Then Paddy lowered her gently down into the deep, short grave and shovelled the soft brown earth in over her. Gradually the blanket disappeared and the earth formed a second blanket. Slowly the earth drew level with the green turf. She was resting beside her lifelong companion, Lolly, who had been laid to rest under the same rowan tree a few months earlier.

Ten years before, Kate and Lolly had bounded into my world full of youth, exuberance and the joys of life. They were large dogs, jet-black and breathtakingly beautiful. Their stance alone breathed fine lineage. Lolly, with her upright, elegant head and long, widespread, muscular legs, had the bearing of a mountaintop deer. Kate had the typical Doberman hump, but nonetheless bore the look of well-bred superiority. These were two ladies of substance with blue blood flowing through every vein, and papers to match.

At the time, I was battered and stumbling along the grief road after a sudden family death and trying desperately to rebuild my broken world. As if sensing my vulnerability, Kate and Lolly immediately took charge of the house and garden. By day they patrolled the yard and garden, quickly establishing the whole area as cat- and rat-free zones. Come darkness, they retired to the kitchen and stretched out in their baskets by the Aga. At the first indication from me that bedtime was approaching, they headed for the back door and scoured their outside territory for unwelcome guests.

On returning indoors, Lolly headed for the stairs and settled into her overnight resting place outside my bedroom door while Kate, having inspected the upstairs corridors, took up her station inside a front bedroom window from where she surveyed the village street. A few hours later, she could be heard thumping down the stairs to her bed by the Aga. By then she had satisfied herself that the upstairs territory was to her satisfaction, so she handed responsibility for that area over to Lolly and went downstairs to her own territory. Kate was the older of the two and the boss.

Over the following months, they inadvertently introduced me to my strongest weapon in coping with grief. Because Dobermans have in their breed greyhound genes, they are constantly on the move and prone to racing, simply for the sheer joy of the speed involved. The result was that in a short time they turned my fine lawns into ploughed fields. Drastic gardening action was required. The lawns had to go! They had to be dug up and replaced by meandering flower beds and wandering paths, all of which had to be immune to destruction from two large, energetic dogs in full flight.

So began the Big Dig, during which I discovered the amazing healing power of digging the earth. During the following months, the dogs and I transformed the garden. As the lawns disappeared, the constant digging calmed and sustained my spirit. Plants that previously had to restrain themselves in limited space were now able to stretch out in a new-found liberty. Gravelled runways were laid down along Kate and Lolly's already formed paths, which resulted in a criss-cross maze of unplanned pathways which moved in a series of unexpected twist and turns, resulting in a far more interesting garden than previously. It was a dog-designed garden! Garden furniture had to be of the solid variety or it would otherwise be upended by dogs in flight. One day, Kate and I happened to be at the top end of the long, sloping garden, when something down at the bottom end caught her attention and she took off, literally sailing through the air like a deer in full flight over shrubs, steps – anything in her way. It made me realise what a powerful animal she was. She tried to dominate Lolly, and when she went a step too far I had to intervene as arbitrator, with the kitchen brush as a threat. To her credit, she never challenged my authority and always backed down without even a growl in my direction.

When a visit to the vet for their annual injections came around, Paddy, who is a farmer, would come with his van and they would jump on board. They loved Paddy, who often told me that if reincarnation was a reality he wanted to come back as Kate and Lolly, as he believed they had the Good Life. On arrival at the veterinary clinic I was always glad of the notice instructing owners to bring their cats in a basket and dogs on a lead, otherwise I feared a bloodbath in the waiting room. Kate and Lolly did not like cats or small dogs, and we always had to hold them firmly under control with strong leads. However, to my relief, they invariably ignored the waiting clientele as if they were beneath their attention. And when Gavin, the vet, opened his surgery door, they paraded into his inner sanctum like military veterans and took their injections like old soldiers. He always remarked how amazingly docile they were for such formidable-looking dogs.

Over the years, Kate and Lolly became part of the fabric of our home and family, and everyone loved them. They gloried in all the love and attention and were part of every family gathering. For Christmas parties they sported two bright red collars with two big red bows. Once the winter fire was lit in the '*seomra ciúin*', as we call our family room, they abandoned

their baskets by the Aga and stretched out in front of the fire. In full stretch they covered such a large section of the floor that we had to step carefully over and around them.

Then a family event came to test them in a new way. A baby grandchild arrived on the scene, and, as the parents were awaiting the completion of their new house, which was just around the corner, they moved into Kate and Lolly's domain. We all watched developments with caution. Kate and Lolly were mildly curious, but no more. When, however, little Ellie got on her feet and toddled around them, they were at first a little nervous and bemused, and then gradually accepting. As Ellie grew firmer on her feet, a loving bond formed between her and the two dogs, and they shared the same floor space. When eventually they all made it together out into the garden, Ellie learned to stand back in case Kate would suddenly take off and knock her sideways. One of Ellie's first sentences was to declare, 'Kate is rough.'

Lolly was Ellie's favourite, as indeed she was mine. She was a gentle, loving, docile dog and maybe the fact that Kate was inclined to dominate her made me more protective of her. Suddenly, in midsummer 2014, Lolly developed a lame leg, which necessitated a visit to Gavin, who prescribed medication. When, after a week the leg had not improved, he advised an X-ray and further investigation. There was something in his demeanour that alerted me to the fact that he felt that all was not well with Lolly.

When the phone call came, the news was bad. Lolly had a cancerous tumour in her hip joint, and the bone was in a bad way. It was up to me to decide on a course of action. Very kindly, Gavin suggested I take a little time and said that he would ring back. There really was no choice. Dobermans are free spirits, and one could not imagine Lolly hobbling around on three legs with no guarantee that the cancer was not progressing.

Paddy and I collected Lolly's body, which we could not bring back to our garden where Kate was waiting for her return. So we took her to Paddy's farm at Farnagow where we laid her to rest under a newly planted rowan tree in their garden.

When Lolly did not return, Kate went into deep mourning and stood in the garden with bowed head and refused to eat. And on every visit Ellie enquired, 'Where is Lolly?' But gradually life returned to normal, and we all got used to life without Lolly. Kate recovered and then took centre stage and lapped up all the extra attention.

However, Kate's days too were numbered, and when she developed a lame leg it sent out red-alert signals. She did at first respond to treatment, and I thought that we were out of the woods. Then, one night when I left her out for her nightly run, she spotted a cat and took off at high speed. When I returned to let her back in, she was clung to the ground in agony. A dreadful pain-filled night ensued and a return visit to Gavin for an X-ray. An enormous fracture showed up. Her age and the condition of her bones were stacked against her recovery, so the inevitable decision had to be made again.

Now Kate and Lolly are both resting under the rowan tree on a hilltop overlooking the village. For ten years they had filled our lives with exuberance, love and delight, for which I am very grateful.

Eventually I will contemplate interviewing replacement candidates – a huge challenge for me and the potential replacements. They will have huge paws to fill!

Chapter 4

Poor Me

I t was raining. Would it ever again stop bloody raining? I was having a 'poor me' day. That can happen in January. I am not a January person. I dragged myself out of bed but it was too wet to go for a walk and I was too lazy to begin taking down the Christmas decorations, which by now, like myself, were beginning to look the worse for wear. I could write, but was not in the mood. Could paint, but did not have the motivation. Could read, but did not have the inclination. I dragged myself around the house for a few hours like a wet blanket. Needing a good kick in the 'you-know-where', I peered out through the front window and gleaned from the lack of wipers in action on passing cars that the rain was taking a break.

I forced myself out the back door. The backyard was covered in a dark green slime after weeks of non-stop rain. Not a cheerful sight. But in the tubs the daffodils, God bless them, were thrusting their green noses above the ground. Now, with no dogs around, they were safe from being upended by nosey Kate. Still, despite these misdemeanours, I missed Kate and Lolly so much. Dogs know when you are having a bad day and love you into a better place.

In the yard, I checked the roses planted at the bases of a home-made arch that I had cobbled together last summer. A strong black pipe arched from one big tub to another. My grand idea was to create an entrance from the front section of the yard to the back corner. Now, Uncle Jacky had never in his life bought an arch for his garden but always made his own. His thinking was why buy it when you can enjoy making it yourself? Fallen trees and branches were turned into garden gates or arches. He loved working with wood, and it gave his garden a blend of harmonious togetherness. I am trying to imitate him and hope that in time the pipe will be smothered into invisibility by the roses. I had planted two Compassion roses in each tub. Two – to be sure to be sure! I am a real Doubting Thomas of gardening and am always delightedly surprised when things actually grow.

Tiny, tentative buds were indeed thrusting forth on the rose stems. That was encouraging. I already had a Compassion rose in the garden and she had proved her worth. In the

past I have bought flaunting flamboyant floozies on impulse and later discovered their lack of dependability. I have learnt my gardening lessons the hard way. So now I give space only to tried and trusted friends. I visualise a mesmerising arch of Compassion here next summer. Gardening is all about anticipatory visualisation. With this possibility in mind, I am already beginning to feel a little bit better.

I stand at the garden gate and watch the birds cling to the feeders. Oh those damned crows! They swoop down and I shoo them away but frighten the little birds in the process. I'm glad that some of the feeders are surrounded by cage protectors that withstand the crows' attacks. As I walk along the path, a gorgeous whiff soothes my senses. The leaves of my beautiful Daphne 'Jacqueline Postill' are glistening with rain, but still her little pink flowers are filling the air with a wonderful scent. She is like manna in the desert, though not wasting her sweetness on the desert air. I inhale deeply, and she comforts my soul.

Then the rain spatters a comeback, and I head for the back door. I slow down to admire a load of logs brought to me at the beginning of winter by Paddy, who was clearing a site for a new milking parlour and had to cut down some trees. On a cold day in November he had spilled out a trailer-load of logs at my back door. What a gift! That is one of the blessings of village living in the midst of a farming community. Farmers make great neighbours. Is there anything more soothing to the senses or promising of warm days ahead than a load of logs? These were organised neatly by young Dan, who had come the day after his father's delivery and stacked them. His grandfather had planted the trees, his father had delivered them, and he had come to stack them. When Dan was born, his family had marked his arrival with the planting of a tree. Trees are a long-lasting mark of a special occasion and an enrichment of people, land and the environment.

As the rain turns from a hesitant drip into a pelting pour, I gather up an armful of logs and head in the back door. I carry the logs to the *seomra ciúin* and light the fire. Recently I have come across natural firelighters that make lighting the fire a pleasurable experience as they emit a scent that blends with the kindling. The turf and logs soon take on a warm glow. I sit and listen to them. They whisper and reach out to me. They talk to me and slowly bring me comfort. My inner icicles begin to thaw. Sitting by a log fire on a wet January evening is a comforting cure for a 'poor me' day. Tomorrow will be a good day.

Chapter 5

Rejuvenation Time

Today I raked the sodden shroud of winter off my garden. Autumn leaves had covered the flower beds with a multicoloured blanket, and later winter frost and rains had saturated them into a thick grey coat, thus shielding the baby growth beneath from stunting winter cold. But now spring was here, and the time had come to peel back the covering coat and discover if any wonders had taken place. During dormant days of winter, miracles can happen beneath the earth. And, yes, there were miracles! Tentative shoots of snowdrops, daffodils and tulips were peeping up through the brown earth. Brave young shoots facing a bright new world. The delight of beholding them brought joy to my heart. All day, as the unveiling took place, a deep peace filled my soul.

There are no words to explain the tranquillity of working with the earth. It is a meditation, a healer and a comforter.

As the hours went by, memories of my father seeped into my mind. Every spring he climbed the steep hill to the Brake Field with his workhorses, Paddy and James. After a winter of relaxation they were full of restless energy and eager to get going. My father wore strong, heavy, leather hobnailed boots, with thick leather soles reinforced by studs and iron clips. They were laced well above his ankles beneath warm wool trousers, and the boots were further extended by a pair of waterproof gaiters that wrapped around his trouser legs and came down over the tops of the boots. Ploughing could be a muddy job.

Inside the gap in the field he pulled the plough out of the ditch where it had rested since the previous year. A plough was a very simple piece of machinery requiring little maintenance except oiling and a quick tightening of joints. This was the implement that connected my father to the earth that was the first step in giving us our daily bread.

Once Paddy and James were hitched to the plough, man and horse balanced themselves in harmony and the first sod was cut by the nose of the plough right up through the middle of the field. As the belly of the dark brown earth fell over, it formed a rich contrast to the vivid green of the spring field. Slowly, my father and his horses worked up and down the long, high field and the opening sod formed a brown ruff along the furrow. As they continued up and down the field, the ruff grew wider. My father angled the plough to achieve a balanced ruff, making sure that each sod rested evenly beside its companion. Along the top of the dark brown earth, long worms squirmed for shelter as crows swooped behind the plough. This was gourmet dining for them! All day the work continued to the background music of cawing crows, the occasional mooing of cows on the hill across the river and the braying of Bill's donkey in the valley below.

Late in the afternoon I came with an enamel jug of tea that had thick slices of buttered brown bread resting across the top. After the climb up the hilly fields I stood at the gap to rest and view the scene. Dusk had softened the field into muted shades of browns and greys, and man and horses were silhouetted against the darkening sky. The crows, cows and donkey had all gone home. Silence prevailed. I sensed a sacred scene. Before me, God, man and nature were blended into one.

I walked slowly across the crumbling clods, breathing in the rich, moist smell of newly turned earth until I reached the headland beside my father and the horses. He joined me on the grass verge, and, as the released horses grazed along the headland, my father sat on an abandoned rolling stone, to be used later to level the field, drank from the enamel jug of tea and savoured my mother's brown bread. He looked down over the shadowing fields and observed changes in the landscape, and he examined the darkening sky forecasting tomorrow's weather. There was about him a different aura. He was by nature an impatient, quick-thinking man, but after hours out in the field ploughing, he seemed to evolve into a kind of meditative monk. I found the profound change deeply moving. Something in my father at this time gave me a new appreciation of the inner man who was often stifled beneath the hardship of eking out a living on a hilly farm on the Cork–Kerry border, where often money was scarce and life hard and demanding. But beneath all the hardship a quiet poet of a man sheltered.

As I waited for my father to finish ploughing, I walked along by the ditch and searched for shamrock, as he'd instructed, but in the dusk it was difficult to differentiate between shamrock and clover. At this time of year, my father was always on the lookout for good bunches of shamrock to be picked and posted to America. They were dispatched in small green boxes bearing an image of St Patrick and the emblem of the shamrock, and probably arrived at their destinations a bit battered by the journey. But for the emigrants they were a precious little bit of home. My father and mother never forgot the people who had emigrated.

When it was too dark to continue the work, he slipped the chains off the horses, who shook themselves free and trotted home beside us with their draped traces clinking against their wide leather collars. My father's boots and gaiters were covered up to his knees with heavy, caked mud, and as he walked along he left clods on the field behind him. At the gap he used the high grass to rid himself of some of the mud. Back in the yard the horses' legs were brushed clean, and they were led to the spout at the bottom of the yard where I was always amazed by the amount of water they could suck up in one giant slug. Then they were led into the stable where they sank their heads into a manger of mangels and sweet-smelling hay. They had earned their reward.

Weeks later, Paddy, James and my father returned to the Brake Field to harrow the sods that by then the frost had crumbled and rendered more pliable. The harrow, like a giant centipede of many claws, scrambled the sods into a soft sea of earth.

Then my father waited for a bright spring day when he brought the corn drill into action. For most of the year, this complex bit of machinery sheltered safely in a dusty farm shed where it lay shrouded in cobwebs. Now it came into its own. It was a long, narrow, wooden box about two foot deep and six foot long, the length of a prone man. When lifted up, the hinged cover revealed a row of holes along the base from where flexible funnels carried the seed down narrow tubes into the earth. To the front was one long, narrow shaft, and the two horses were tackled on either side. They drew the corn drill to the prepared field where my father had bags of wheat, oats and barley seeds in readiness. The drill cover was raised, a full bag of seed was poured in, and the horses were guided carefully up and down the field. My father walked along behind the drill and controlled the rate of grain flowing into the soft earth with a little lever. By evening, the Brake Field was pregnant with seed. Then the rolling stone emerged from the ditch, and Paddy was back in action on his own, as this was a one-horse job. The rolling stone was the length of Mick Jagger, and the whole field was rolled over till it was flat and even. Sometimes, in order to deter the crows from helping themselves, scarecrows were erected around the field, though I felt that the crows were not often convinced by that.

Man and horse had completed their task. Now it was up to God and nature.

Oh brown ploughed field
What an ancient skill
Is in your turned sod,
A skill inherited
By generations of earthy men.
You cover the hillside
In a cloak of brown velvet;
What a richness is yours.
You are an open book
Yet to be written;

The virginity of the upturned sod
Waiting to be fertilised
By the hands of man
And nurtured by the warmth of nature.

Within a few weeks, the wonder of green shoots began to spread across the wide field, and as they emerged a light run-over with the rolling stone fortified them against crows. Slowly the varying shades of the different crops turned the Brake Field into a patchwork quilt. Beyond the grain were long drills of potatoes, cabbage, turnips and mangels that we children, wearing hemp bags as knee protectors, had helped to plant into little beds of farmyard manure that had been drawn by Paddy and James in a timber butt to the fields. The Brake Field was our food cupboard for the coming year.

The wheat would go to the mills to be ground into flour to give us our daily bread, the oats crushed for the animals and the barley sold to the brewery for stronger potions. The potatoes, turnips and cabbage found their way onto our table, and the mangels sustained the horses. On Rogation Days, which were spring days of requesting the Lord to take care of our crops, my parents went to the Brake Field and blessed it with holy water.

Now, many years later, as I garden in my own little corner of the earth, I am grateful to my father for those days of ploughing when I caught a glimpse of the man who found God and tranquillity out in the fields. He opened a gate into a world for which I will be forever grateful.

Chapter 6

The Colour
of Memory

As I went in the door of the exclusive boutique, it immediately caught my eye. The rich red of the hawthorn berry, edged in bronze with the amber tones of an autumnal branch, drew me like a magnet. It was love at first sight. It whirled me back to a riverside meadow, a meadow surrounded by a russet hawthorn hedge. The hedge was laden with rich red haws, ripe for picking. Their colour proclaimed their ripeness and they parted easily from the russet branch. My father first rolled them in his farm-mellowed hand then declared them edible. That childhood picture must have been unconsciously stored in a locked drawer at the back of my mind. The sight of the red scarf shot the drawer wide open and the picture danced out. It framed a meadow, my father and the haws. The deep rich colour of the scarf spun the haws around the boutique in a flush of warm welcome.

I had come into the shop to buy a jacket, but the scarf wiped the jacket clean out of my mind. I approached it in awe and gingerly ran my fingers along its downy softness. It felt just like the *ceannabhán* that wafts in soft puffs across the heather of the bog, the stuff that dreams are made of. This scarf was destined for me. I did, however, gasp a little – well, maybe more than a little – when I saw the price tag. But what price dreams? The scarf was my warm past, my delighted present and my enriched future. You cannot quantify that in monetary terms. Can you?

Decision made, I turned my attention to the jacket, and, by one of those unbelievable chances that can sometimes happen when out shopping, the perfect jacket to match the scarf was on the rail. This was my day! The special occasion up ahead was getting brighter by the minute. However, a suitable blouse or some kind of a top was also needed to go inside the jacket. Unfortunately there was none that hit the spot in my classy boutique or in any other shops in our town. A trip to the big smoke would be necessary.

I brought home my purchases with a triumphant glow. Now, as all women know, when you go on a shopping spree its success is not one hundred percent confirmed until you come back home and parade the purchases in front of your own mirror. I had no question mark over the scarf, but I needed to see the jacket on home turf. It passed the winning post with flying colours, showing off the scarf in triumph.

A few days at home were required to recover after my big spend. During those days I often took the time to feel the beautiful texture of my lovely new scarf, admire its spirit-enriching colour and simply wallow in its beauty. My mother had loved beautiful materials, and it was always a joy to watch her appreciate the texture and weave of a good fabric. She would have loved this scarf – but she would probably have got a heart attack at the price! But for me to have my father *and* mother remembered in one scarf was just amazing.

Then, bright and early one morning, when my scarf was just four days old, I boarded the bus to Cork. My scarf was on its first outing. I was wearing it to act as a colour guide for the required top to match the new jacket. I did the rounds of many shops, good, bad and indifferent, but there was no colour match for my scarf. Finally, my decision-making capabilities collapsed, and, in need of sustenance, I retired to a city-centre restaurant to water the horses and restore my equilibrium. This restaurant was a cathedral of gourmet food. I was feeling self-indulgent. After all, I was mentally dancing in a wildflower meadow full of glowing poppies and rich red haws. This was a day for taking time to smell the roses! In my restful restaurant, I savoured a feast of cholesterol-enriching dishes. I ate well, but not wisely. In the throes of this satisfying of the senses I found it desirable to remove my jacket and in the process readjusted my beloved scarf around my neck. Repast complete, I donned my jacket and left the restaurant.

Back on the street, I realised instantly and to my absolute horror that I was without my scarf! It must have slipped off when I was putting on my jacket. I rushed back into the restaurant, glad to have realised so quickly that the scarf was missing and expecting to see it strewn across the table or piled up on the floor. There was no trace of it. I looked around in alarm. Where could it possibly have gone in such a short time? The diners at the next table had their backs to my table and were totally engrossed in their conversation.

Then inspiration struck – the waitress must have picked it up and put it safely aside under the desk awaiting my return. My panic subsided. I sought out the waitress who had served me, confident that she had the solution to my problem. She looked at me blankly. Was I sure that I had a scarf? Her reaction set me back: she simply could not but have noticed that scarf. Her next question! Could I have dropped it in the street outside? I quickly realised that I was on a boat to nowhere. I left my name and phone number in case it was handed in but sensed that I was in a no-win saloon.

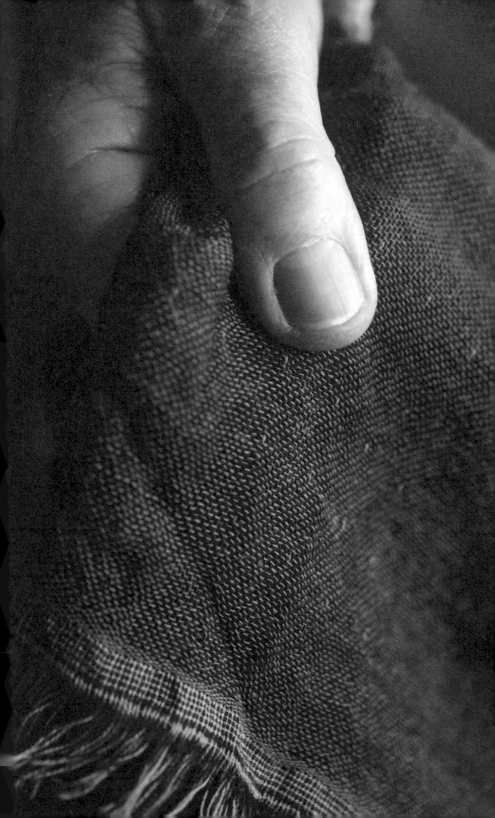

My sunny day suddenly turned grey. My glowing poppies wilted and my plump, scarlet haws shrank. The city streets were no longer warm and inviting. It was time to go home. I needed the comfort of my own place. I knew that my beloved scarf had been in that restaurant when I left, so somebody must have simply picked it up and pocketed it. Such happenings, I know, are probably a regular occurrence, but when they happen to you they break your trust in the goodness of your fellow human beings.

With no further desire to shop, I trudged to the bus and arrived home in a deflated state. I put on the kettle and made tea and toast. I did not need tea and toast, but the ritual of tea-making is soothing for a bruised spirit, and warm toast and honey has always been my comfort food. I rang the restaurant to be told sharply that I must have lost my scarf in the street outside because if it had fallen in the restaurant none of their clientele would have touched it. They were not that kind of people! I felt intimidated by the strident tone and decided that was that, there was no more to be done. I had to accept my beating. That's the way life is.

The following day dawned bright and beautiful. It was one of those golden autumn days that God sends to get us through winter. Re-energised, I rang my boutique to be told that, yes, they had another scarf in stock. My mother would definitely have died of a heart attack at the price of *two* such scarves – but, then, she and my father were totally responsible for my mad love affair with the scarf, weren't they?

This scarf is a summer meadow, a glowing russet hedge, a warm brown hand full of red ripe haws and my mother's small, delicate, work-worn hand lovingly savouring the delights of richly woven autumn tweeds. Such a scarf is priceless!

And when I went back to the boutique to collect my gorgeous replacement scarf, an unexpected surprise awaited me: my daughter had already been there and had paid for it! Faith in my fellow human beings was restored. That lovely gesture made the scarf even more valuable.

Chapter 7

Johnny's Skip

A few days ago when I came out my side door, Johnny, who lives across the road, had a skip outside his gate. In our family, we have an old 'skip' photo that makes us all smile: it is a picture that I took many years ago of my long-suffering husband, Gabriel, in the depths of a skip trying to redeem items that I had thrown in. It was taken during a period when I was making one of my many feeble efforts to declutter our house. Back then, I could never see myself actually taking things *out* of a skip. But skips can be fascinating places, I must admit. Johnny was looking into his skip, surveying its contents, when I joined him.

'What are you clearing out now?' I enquired, as Johnny is constantly clearing and rebuilding on his premises behind

his pub. 'There's a beautician moving in upstairs,' he told me, pointing to the top windows of his house above the hairdresser's. 'Great,' I told him, 'a beautician will be good for the village.' Good for me, too, I decided privately, as I am now of an age when continuing repairs and maintenance are necessary.

Then something in the skip caught my eye. 'Johnny, why are you throwing out those fine earthenware flowerpots?' I protested. 'Take them if you want to,' he told me, grinning at my foolishness. 'And anything else you'd fancy as well. Or if you need to get rid of anything, now is your time. Throw it in there. This skip will be here until Tuesday.'

Johnny disappeared, and I helped myself to the pots. I continued to inspect the skip. It is very interesting to look in and see what people throw into skips. In here was a couch that to me looked perfectly usable, and I thought what a shame to throw that out; there were also quite a few small cabinets that looked in good condition. *Alice, go in home now and mind your own business*, I told myself firmly, *you already have enough rubbish in your house.*

Still, I kept my eye on the skip. Surely somebody would retrieve that couch? Covered in soft, pink, crushed velvet, it seemed to invite conversation and relaxation. But the couch remained there one whole day, with one arm hoisted forlornly to the sky. Before going to bed that night, I looked out my bedroom window which overlooks Johnny's back gate and regretted that the couch was still there. Hopefully it would not rain overnight and ruin it. When I got up the following morning, I forgot to look out the window and check on the couch, but when I came out my door I was delighted to see that it was gone. *Good for you*, I thought, imagining the lucky new owner. That was a great find and to get it for nothing was jam – and jam up on it. Then I began to wonder about the rest of the contents. The cabinets? Surely someone could find a use for them. They remained for another two days. Then, finally, they too disappeared. I never saw anybody take them, but one by one they were gone until the skip contained only real rubbish. It all made great sense. Maybe we are beginning to catch up with our Continental neighbours who put their surplus outside their house and when people have helped themselves, the remainder gets taken by the City Fathers. An ideal system.

I would sorely need to apply that system to my house, but while I am still up and running it will never happen. The day after my demise six skips will probably be lined up the hill outside the house and my offspring will be flinging stuff into them for a whole week! I hope then that people will come and help themselves to the varied collection of objects that I have accumulated over the years. Clocks, for example.

I have always loved clocks. Maybe it springs from the reverence that my father had for the one clock that we had in our old farmhouse. It hung on the kitchen wall and kept exact time as he had perfected the difficult skill of subtly adjusting the brass pendulum that controlled the timing mechanism. There was a tiny lever beneath the pendulum, and the slightest twist in one direction or another would either speed things up or slow them down. There was a pencil mark down the wall beside the clock, and that was the 'shipping line' outside which the clock was not to travel. When the wall was being distempered, he issued ultimatums about the dire consequences of moving the clock. If his daughters insisted that this drastic step simply had to be taken, he declared that he alone was capable of making the move. He introduced into this undertaking all the drama of moving the *Mona Lisa*. One of my irreverent sisters once whispered sarcastically, as he stage-managed this performance, 'You'd think that we were taking Christ down off the cross.'

First he ceremoniously opened the little glass door at the front as if he was opening a tabernacle. Then he gently stilled the swinging pendulum. Next he crouched down and peered up into the lower regions of the clock to ascertain the exact point at which the pendulum was attached to the main works. Then he gently eased the pendulum off that hook and carried it across the kitchen as if he was bearing the Ardagh Chalice. He ceremoniously laid it on top of the old battery radio on the window, which he judged to be the only place safe from fussy females and children who constantly kept his blood pressure at boiling point. Then he returned to the now gaping-mouthed clock and gently closed the little door like a loving relative closing the mouth of the recently deceased. Finally he raised both hands heavenwards as if seeking divine intervention and lovingly took his clock down off the wall and held it at arm's length. Like a high priest, he then proceeded out the kitchen door and up into the parlour with one of his daughters like John the Baptist preparing the way by running ahead and opening doors. Then the clock was laid reverently in the centre of the parlour table, and he ran his hands gently over it as if reassuring his precious clock that all would be well until he returned.

My clocks get no such reverential treatment, and if I want to slow down or speed up the tempo I have to try hard to remember in which direction I need to twist the tiny lever – if the clock is racing ahead the following day, I know that I have got it wrong. Whether they are going fast or slow, though, the ticking of those old clocks is soothing to the spirit. One is never alone in a room with a ticking clock. And like everything old they require a certain amount of loving care, including a weekly wind-up. Forget your clock, and she will give you the silent treatment.

One of these clocks had come out of a skip when an old neighbour spotted it and presented it to me with the comment, 'Missus, you are into all kinds of rubbish.' To be honest, it did look a bit rubbishy as it was clothed in varied coats of many colours of paint but after careful denuding it revealed a body of rich mahogany embossed with occasional mother-of-pearl. Who would not love it?

More vocal than the ticking clock is the chiming mantel clock, of which I have three. Yes, three! But now comes the justification. One I inherited from Uncle Jacky. He was given it when he got married in 1932 by the Valley Rovers GAA club of which he was chairman. It took up duty immediately in the post office where it became the village clock to be checked regularly by schoolchildren, bus catchers and Mass-goers. It is now on the mantelpiece over the fire in the *seomra ciúin* and unfortunately the years have slowed it down. Unlike the wall clocks, however, this lady has no visible apparatus for controlling the time. She is mistress of her own rate of progress into the future. Another mantel clock was a wedding present to one of my children from an antique-loving uncle, but this child of the modern world has yet to mature into an appreciation of such things. So it remains with me on a large sideboard inherited from Aunty Peg. This sideboard is the home of many things that came with it and others that have since joined them.

Then, one day, while traversing an antique shop and praying for the power to resist its contents, a distant clock pealed out the Big Ben chimes, a beautiful, mellow, melodious sound. I grew up listening to that sound on the BBC as my father waited for the six o'clock news to hear how the rest of the world was managing without him. That clock, of course,

came home with me. Years later, when I was chatting on the phone to my daughter in Boston, the clock began to chime in the background, and my daughter said nostalgically, 'Oh, that's the sound of home.'

Then I have a grandfather clock, which I actually forgot to include until last and is now peering reproachfully at me from across the room. We bought it to mark the Millennium. It did not cost a fortune as it's a bit battered and not a creation of immense beauty. And I did nothing to improve its appearance when I shifted it awkwardly for a decorating job and its head fell off and rolled along the floor. This resulted in a permanent tilt of the head so that it now looks as if it is acknowledging you as you enter the room. But, strangely enough, despite its not very impressive appearance, it is a perfect timekeeper. I keep it ticking but not chiming, because unfortunately it does not have the voice of an angel but rather the hoarse rasp of a dying frog. So the vocal cords are never wound up.

My father would have loved winding it as it's a bit of a performance. First you retrieve the tiny key off the timber lip that separates the face from the long body. Having opened his front waistcoat with the small key, you then go back to the lip for an odd-looking key that is inserted into his face below his cheekbones, and you laboriously turn this strong key as the clock shudders in protest. While you are doing this, a large weight slowly jerks its way upwards in his inner regions. Then you swing the pendulum into motion. The other weight is for the chimer, but I do not wind that up, so he remains silent. Then I lock him up, and he keeps going for a week.

My clocks depend on me to keep them ticking, and over the years we have become old friends. Undoubtedly they do contribute to the clutter – though not as much as the books. But that is another story.

Chapter 8

The Split

A laid-back Canadian cousin visited us and the All Ireland Hurling Final happened to be on TV. It was his first time in Ireland, so we pulled out all the stops to make a good impression. First, he had enjoyed a pleasant, sociable meal around the kitchen table as part of an extended family gathering. Afterwards, we sat chatting and exchanging family news. All was going well. Then it was time for the match. Cork were playing in the final.

There was a mass movement, which included him, into the large front room where the TV resides. Our visitor was full of curiosity about the game as he had never seen a hurling match, not to mind an All Ireland Hurling Final. We gave him the best seat in the house and the rest of us settled ourselves comfortably around the room, with the overflow and the flexible relegated to the floor. He sat back in expectation of a relaxing afternoon's entertainment and may even have harboured a faint hope of popcorn accompanied by an introductory analysis. Things went calmly for the first few minutes, and, conscious of our guest, decorum prevailed.

Then Cork scored a goal, and the room erupted in mayhem. As the game progressed, the fortunes of Cork rose, crashed and rose again. With each Cork score we abandoned our chairs, danced around the floor and were transported up to Croke Park, where we jumped and shrieked in ecstasy. Chairs were cast aside with yells of delight and showers of praise were poured on the triumphant. When near misses came, we hurled verbal missiles of abuse at the culprits. Previous heroes quickly became villains. We were no longer in a room in Innishannon but around a Roman arena, rising and falling with the tide of execution. We forgot about our uninitiated cousin, who by now had shrunk into the background. With a Cork victory and the final war dance completed, we came back down to earth.

'That was amazing!' the Canadian breathed. 'Yes, 'twas a great game, wasn't it?' we enthused, assuming he was referring to the game. 'Not the game,' he gasped, 'you guys were unbelievable. If you did that back home you would all be locked up.' Would we? We were taken aback.

The GAA is an unexplainable Irish phenomenon. It is

tribal to the core and is rooted in every parish in Ireland. Amongst its members are the idealist, the martyr to the cause, the armchair expert, the fanatic, the thick, the thud and the normal human being. It is the backbone of most parishes and for years has channelled male aggression into hurleys, balls and opponents. It is an outlet for unreleased energy and budding male testosterone. And now the ladies have entered the pitch and are gaining ground fast.

Politics and the GAA have a lot in common, and sooner or later in both arenas 'the split' is inevitable. Here in Innishannon, during my village tenure, I have witnessed a few splits in our local club, the Valley Rovers, and because I married into a GAA family I always had a ringside seat.

The first split was a little before my time, but the debris was still afloat when I came to the village. It had to do with the purchase of the pitch. Buying land in Ireland seldom goes without complications, and the more people involved in the process the more complicated it becomes. The biggest problems arise when you have an owner but also a renter, who, over time, evolves into a self-perceived owner. John B. Keane illustrated this dilemma spellbindingly in *The Field* where The Bull, over years of use, had fallen in love with 'his' field even though it was actually owned by The Widow. The same thing happened in Innishannon, and when the owner of a suitable field decided to sell and the Valley Rovers decided to buy, conflict arose. This field was known as The Bleach. Its

name comes from an earlier usage. A former landowner in Innishannon, Thomas Adderley, was an entrepreneur, and he brought over a community of French Huguenots who were fleeing religious persecution in France; they were wonderful craftspeople, and using their skills he set up a silk and linen industry. They bleached the linen in a large field along by the river behind his house, and this field is still known as The Bleach. This was now the bone of contention. For the GAA it was ideally placed, right in the centre of the village.

The Valley Rovers felt that they could not pass up the opportunity of a village pitch. The purchasers were dubbed the 'valley grabbers' by some people. My husband's Uncle Jacky was involved in the purchase, but because he was a walking saint he could not cope with conflict. His wife, Aunty Peg, had to man the defences. While the conflict was in full flow and she felt the occasion necessitated it, she would take an opponent by the scruff of the neck and reverse him out her shop door. Aunty Peg was no lightweight and certainly no pushover! After a certain amount of local 'tally ho', the deal was completed, things eventually settled down and normality again prevailed. Uncle Jacky was happy to pass on The Bleach endeavours to the next generation.

Years later, a mini split arose when a local team – against the wishes of the then chairman – were taken to a local brewery to celebrate a win. Direct honesty can sometimes land you into a whole pile of trouble, and when the chairman, never renowned for beating around the bush, stood up in the brewery and told the large gathering, including the brewery heavyweights, that this was no place to bring an under-age team for celebrations, he set the cat among the pigeons. Today, ministers of state are still struggling to disentangle the drink and sporting businesses and it is still proving a sticky problem.

The next split was over money. My father always said that you only really got to know people when you had land or money dealings with them. Fund-raising is an ongoing challenge for all voluntary organisations, and down through the years the Valley Rovers were no exception. One big fund-raising project of raffling a car crashed lamentably when the money disappeared in a swirl of smoke and mirrors. The committee knew where it had gone but were powerless to retrieve it, and, of course, recriminations were not scarce in forthcoming: 'Ye should have known better.' 'What fools ye were.' All the armchair experts had a field day!

In recent years, when the latest split came, we were back to landownership again. It proved extremely difficult to get to the root of this latest split. Like everything else in life, even splits have got more complicated. One portion of the club judged that another portion was planning to build on The Bleach. The Bleach is holy ground in the village, and even the murmur of such a thought was enough to cause convulsions. But the standing officers refuted the claim: it was a false rumour, they maintained. Still, even false rumours can bring down governments, and so it brought down the Valley Rovers club officers, who resigned en masse. It took a couple of years to recover from that convulsion, but with time everything is forgiven and forgotten – though maybe never *quite* forgotten! That is village living.

Chapter 9

The Parish Picnic

It was early morning in Dromkeen Wood. The birds were welcoming the new day with an enthusiastic chorus of delight. Climbing up the steep incline, it was good to breathe in the musky smell of moist bluebells that stretched all around in a carpet of blue. It was Bluebell Day, and the wood was telling the story.

Over the centuries, Innishannon has had a chequered history of occupation and struggle. The wood too has a history. In 1750, the landlord, Thomas Adderley, planted this wood. The man who then managed the Adderley estate was a maternal ancestor of the well-known actor Jeremy Irons; this fact came to light when Jeremy Irons did a programme called *Who Do You Think You Are?* a few years ago on BBC

TV. After the Adderleys came the Frewens, who took down the Adderley riverside mansion and rebuilt it on a more elevated site above the village with a beautiful view down along the river valley and looking across to the Adderley Wood, which the Frewens promptly replanted and renamed the Frewen Wood. To get the full picture of the Frewens, it is necessary to travel back along the female line, which can sometimes be more intriguing than the male. This particular family tree was made very interesting indeed by its colourful ladies. They were posh high flyers who spent money like water. The well-researched book *Fortune's Daughters* tells the story of these extraordinary women. The three beautiful Jerome sisters came from New York, and their family was dripping in riches, but they lacked blue blood, a fact that their social-climbing mother was determined to change. To remedy the situation, she took her daughters to Paris in search of blue-blooded husbands, and when Paris failed to provide the needful she brought them to London for 'the season'. There they acquired the desired husbands, but unfortunately did not marry firstborn sons, which would have guaranteed inheritance rights that by now were necessary as their father, through bad investments and extravagance, had seen a sudden collapse in their fortunes.

Jenny, the most beautiful of the sisters, married Randolph Churchill, the youngest son of the Duke of Marlborough, and became the mother of Winston Churchill. Leonie married into the Leslies, a distinguished Irish family, and Clara married Mortimer Frewen, who, as the result of a financial exchange with the Adderleys, now owned Innishannon.

In Innishannon, Mortimer Frewen set up a fish hatchery, which was very advanced thinking for the time, and the area beside the bridge where he sited it is still known as The Hatchery. Because of Mortimer's many financial disasters the Frewens were constantly without cash flow, though this did not impinge on their high-flying lifestyle. Eventually, due to the changing face of politics in Ireland, they left Innishannon for good and in later years many of the village homeowners bought out their ground rent from the Frewen estate. This was often a very complicated and time-consuming procedure. The landlord system in Ireland left many deep-seated and painful after-effects, but the two positives were great houses and great trees.

Thus the Adderley Wood was renamed Frewen Wood, but it is now called Dromkeen Wood, and is the property of Coillte, the Irish State body. Owners may come and go, but trees and wildlife go on regardless of mere mortals. Dromkeen Wood has always been a haven of delight for the people of Innishannon, and the village children spend hours playing here and in the stream that tumbles down the rocky incline near the entrance. Beside the wood was once the village forge, where Billy the Blacksmith, as well as shoeing horses, performed many other functions. When village children were going to the wood, their parents would instruct them, 'Tell Billy that you are there,' knowing that he would keep a supervisory eye on them. The forge was also a male social club where the local farmers gathered at night to discuss the state of the nation. They called it the Dáil, and Billy always said that far more intelligent discussions were held there than in the actual Dáil. Now Billy is long gone, and the village that loved him erected a sculpture of him at the entrance to the restored old forge that is now all smartened up and the office of an architectural firm.

In recent years, the paths and steps in Dromkeen Wood have deteriorated, so we in the village decided that it was time to improve things and to install handrails for the less flexible. We were grant-aided by the Gwendoline Harold-Barry Trust, Cork County Council, Merck, Sharp and Dohme, and Eli Lilly. The work was carried out and supervised by Coillte. When all was completed, we decided to celebrate the transformation with a big thank you to our benefactors and a parish picnic. Bluebell Day was to be parish picnic day.

I had the wood to myself that morning, and it was a glorious morning. Sunlight slanted through the trees and birds darted along the branches. Suddenly a flick of red caught my eye and brought me to a standstill. A gorgeous fluffy-tailed red squirrel shot up a tree just beside me – it was a native squirrel, a species unfortunately now in danger from the imported grey. The quick glimpse of this beautiful creature filled me with a rush of joy. So seldom seen and so beautiful! Patrick Kavanagh captured well the delight of such a rare experience when he wrote, 'Through a chink too wide there comes in no wonder.' At that moment I understood perfectly the sentiment of the poet. Poetry links across the ages when the poet and the rememberer share the same strain of thought. When you experience something that leaves you speechless and the line of a long-forgotten poem sprouts at the back of your brain, you and the poet are on an invisibly connected wavelength. It is magic! And it makes worthwhile the reading and learning of poetry.

The appearance of the squirrel put pep in my step, and I wandered on hoping for another sighting. But it was not to be. Then it was time to head home and get things ready for the picnic. I was loath to leave this restful place behind. As I sauntered slowly down the deep incline I realised that the next step in making this haven more heavenly for wood walkers was a few wooden benches placed in strategic spots from where you could catch a glimpse of the river and the village through a gap in the trees. A seat here and there would also provide a welcome break on the steep climb upwards. The words of another poem, by WH Davies, learnt in school, came back to me:

What is this life if, full of care,
We have no time to stand and stare.

No time to stand beneath the boughs
And stare as long as sheep or cows.

No time to see, when woods we pass,
Where squirrels hide their nuts in grass.

No time to see, in broad daylight,
Streams full of stars, like skies at night.

No time to turn at Beauty's glance,
And watch her feet, how they can dance.

No time to wait till her mouth can
Enrich that smile her eyes began.

A poor life this if, full of care,
We have no time to stand and stare.

Back home, my friends and I packed baskets of food and filled flasks with tea and coffee. We had invited families to bring their own picnic baskets but it is always best to put into practice the slogan of the Boy Scouts and Girl Guides: be prepared. Back in the wood we set up our tables under the trees and awaited the arrivals. The Scouts and Guides were the first to come, stepping in smart formation over the bridge; then, on arrival, they quickly disappeared into the wood. This was familiar territory to them as they use the wood for Scout practice and also keep it litter-free. Then, slowly, people drifted over the bridge from the village, and, when the sponsors were all present we began the ceremony of official thanks. It was a great opportunity for the village to acknowledge and thank our benefactors. The Tidy Towns group was in charge of the speeches and procedures, and the arrival of a soft mist hurried up the proceedings, which were taking place in a little green area on the outskirts of the wood. We finished with a song written and sung by a local man, Jerry Larkin. A man of many talents, who is an artist, musician and singer, he had written this song when we unveiled the sculpture of the Horse and Rider in 2009 at the entrance to the village to honour the people of yesteryear who had walked or travelled on horseback through our village. He sang it again now. The song has a rousing rhythm and completed the formalities on a vibrant note.

The Crossing Song

Well they headed down to Bothairín Átha
And waited till the tide was low,
They headed down to Bothairín Átha
A long, long time ago.

Then they crossed the river at the shallow ford,
Nags 'n' carts and livestock all,
They crossed the river at the shallow ford
And made it without a fall.

And they reached the slipway and travelled on
A trip made o'er and o'er,
Yes, they reached the slipway and travelled on
Till they were safe once more.

Down through the years the route remains,
Down all the days did last,
Now horse and rider standing proud,
Let's celebrate our past.

Then we all gathered into the wood around the laden tables under the trees. The gigantic, fresh-leafed beeches formed perfect translucent green umbrellas. Is there anything better than tea and home-made apple tart under a tree in a wood surrounded by friends and neighbours? The children ran up the deep inclines and then rolled down again, covering themselves in leaf mould. It was a day for all of us to savour the freedom of the woods and enjoy the beauty that surrounds us. Thank you, Mr Adderley, Mr Frewen and our own Coillte.

Chapter 10

The Presbytery

Over the past half-century, an interesting parade of priests has been in and out of our presbytery. One evening, when one of them had vacated it, I walked around the empty house and thought of the many changes it had seen. I wrote this poem.

Vacuum womb house
Contracted into a new life,
An afterbirth remaining
Whispers and shadows
Of another day.
Memory on its
Soft grey clouds

Wafting through the rooms,
Webbing here
The part of me
That belongs
The living that was blended
Through these stones
So I take with me
Part soul of this house
And leave behind
Part of me.

The presbytery is an elegant old house surrounded by gardens, situated behind the church and facing south over Dromkeen Wood. Down through the years the priests who have lived there have either loved, hated or merely tolerated this old house. They, like priests in parishes all around the country, have left their footprints on our parish and in this house and are remembered in different ways by different people.

In the early sixties, Fr Jack Tarbert and his sister, Jess, turned the presbytery from a bachelor pad into a gracious home. They installed an Aga in the spacious kitchen, and Fr Jack, who was a superb carpenter, turned the old coach house into a workshop. An expert gardener specialising in roses, he transformed the gardens behind the church into a magical corner. Jess, who was 'to the manor born', had the presbytery smelling of wax polish and garden flowers. The gracious old building glowed in the midst of rose gardens, and you were met at the door by an aura of good housekeeping, of which Jess was a master. Coming from a mixed religious background with a cousin a Presbyterian minister in the North, they had the Protestant work ethic, and Jess would have made the perfect vicar's wife. If priests were allowed to marry, she would have been an ideal choice. She ran parish bazaars, kept an eye on parish finances, and, as well as being the priest's housekeeper, she was the supervising sacristan and altar-boy manager. In summer, she served visitors tea in china cups accompanied by cucumber sandwiches beneath the extended branches of a beech tree on the lawn.

During his time with us, Fr Jack, assisted by volunteers, erected the grotto at the eastern end of the village. The location was ideal, with natural rock and a flowing stream, but it still required a lot of digging and earth removal. The site was given by adjacent landowner Marie Roche, and the statues of Our Lady and Bernadette were donated by Aunty Peg. It is now a tranquil oasis beside the non-stop traffic flowing through our village into West Cork.

Fr Michael O'Riordan, who came after the Tarberts, was a total contrast. He was a farmer from Kilmichael in West Cork, and with his arrival the roses faded and the cucumber sandwiches were no more. His favourite song was 'The Boys of Kilmichael', celebrating a famous ambush there during the War of Independence, and once, during a rendering of the hymn 'Faith of our Fathers' at a solemn parish event, he aired the opinion that maybe 'The Boys' would be more appropriate. He was very funny, with a witty turn of phrase, and a real rogue. He became known to us all as Fr Mick, and the mention of his name still brings a smile of pleasant remembrance to the faces of those who knew him. A people's person with a great understanding of human nature, he got our parish hall built with voluntary labour, which even in those days was no mean achievement. It still stands today and is much used.

In total contrast was his successor, Fr Seamus Murphy, a reserved, ascetic man, who nevertheless had every young lad in the parish playing hurling and football. He laid the foundation of the Valley Rovers teams that we have today. He believed in good behaviour on and off the pitch and never tolerated foul play. In 1974, he planted a young copper beech beside the church gate, and it is now an impressive presence known as 'Fr Murphy's tree'.

Then came Fr Lucy, who was of the old school, with a housekeeper to match. He evicted intrusive cameras from First Holy Communion rails when it was a very unpopular decision, though years later, when they became an absolute blight, the local Parents' Association endeavoured to do likewise. He did not curry public favour and was rigid in many ways, but he had surprising corners of kindness and understanding. The morning after the Valley Rovers debacle of the missing money he arrived with a cheque and said, 'Let that be the start of the new fund and put behind ye what has happened; it has happened to smarter people than ye.'

Fr O'Donovan then breezed into the parish – a man in a hurry. Yet, on Holy Thursday nights a transformation took place when he slowed down and held a most reverent Holy Hour that brought us all close to the gates of Heaven. He had amazing radio skills and touched a wide audience when he presented *Faith Matters* on local radio. People loved listening to him.

Then came Fr John Kingston, a gentle, reserved man, who renovated our two parish churches at a cost of almost three million euros and never ruffled a parish feather, which could be described as a truly amazing achievement. While the restoration was being carried out we had Mass in the Church of Ireland church, and their congregation came to our church while they were restoring theirs. It was ecumenism in action.

Now we have Fr Finbarr Crowley, who, because he was reared in a pub, has the common touch while still rising splendidly to all occasions. The gracious old parochial house has been restored, and he operates an open-door policy and is available to all at all times. The young are actively involved in church ceremonies, and our congregations are increasing.

These priests, like others all over Ireland, have christened our babies, listened to our troubles, sung at our weddings and buried our dead. Back in the seventies they were regarded as above reproach, which was not good for them or us. In frustration at the dominant position that the Church held in Irish life I wrote the following poem around that time.

Clergyman all dressed in black
What a mighty church is at your back.
We are taught that by your hand
We must be led to our promised land.
Jesus is locked in your institutions
Of ancient laws and resolutions,
Buried so deep and out of sight
Sometimes we cannot see the light,
Behind huge walls that cost so much
Where simple things are out of touch.
But could it be He is not within
These walls so thick with love so thin?
Does He walk on distant hills
Where long ago He cured all ills?
Is He gone to open places
To simple people all creeds all races?
Is Jesus gone from off the altar,
Catching fish down by the water?
Is He with the birds amongst the trees
Gathering honey with the bees?

PRAY FOR THE REPOSE
OF
THE SOUL OF
VERY REV
PATRICK CANON McSWEENEY
PARISH PRIEST OF
INNISHANNON & KNOCKAVILLA
1931 - 1953
DIED 17TH DECEMBER 1953

MAY HE REST IN PEACE.

PARISH PRIEST
OF
INNISHANNON
AND
KNOCKAVILLA
1866 TO 1895.

Could it be in this simple way
That God meant man to kneel and pray?

I showed it to our then curate, Fr Seamus, who smiled sadly and said, 'Alice, did it ever dawn on you that we too are victims of the system?' That put a stop to my judgemental attitude. A few months later, with the advent of the lay ministry, he asked me to join in. I recoiled at first, and he said quietly, 'It is so easy to stand in judgement – but doing something to change the system is the real challenge.' He was right and I accepted his invitation. It is indeed so easy to be Mouth Almighty! Due to the sins of a few, some of our good priests find themselves demeaned and perceived as undesirables. The many ageing priests who, in parishes all around Ireland, dedicated their lives to helping people must find all this very hurtful.

Due to the decline in vocations there are many unavoidable changes on the way. So, while we still have them, let us cherish and appreciate the honourable priests who weathered the volcanos that erupted around them and tried to keep going through terrible times.

Sometimes in life we self-destruct and then a new phoenix rises out of the ashes. At the moment, is that happening in the Church? Are we witnessing a new creation? New creations can be a bit scary, but sometimes can be wonderful.

Chapter 11

The Rising Sun

Bury me at Rosnaree
And face me to the rising sun.

The Travelling People always camped here. In their search for shelter they located the warmest roads of Ireland, and this little road was a cosy corner. Behind them at night the canopy of trees in Dromkeen Wood formed the headboard of their bed, and, facing south-east, they awoke to the morning sun warm on their faces. The great architecturally planned houses of the time were built with their morning rooms facing east to catch the early sunlight, but with far less expense the Travelling People had the same benefits along this little road. In the old days, the guidelines given for deciding on house location came from the wisdom of the natural world. The advice was to watch the cow, who, when the weather came bad, sought the most sheltered corner of a field, turned her rump to the north and faced south. That was the spot and orientation in which to build your house. In today's world we hire feng-shui experts to provide the same wise guidance.

The last resident of this old road was Bridgie Donovan, who often rode in to the village on her High Nelly bike; she died about fifty years ago but the road is still known locally as Bridgie Donovan's road. In the higher circles of society one must achieve greatness to have such an honour bestowed on one, but Bridgie earned this right simply by being the last person to live here.

Far older residents rest here too, people who go much further back in history then Bridgie. For over a hundred and fifty years, in an unmarked hilly field beside this road, many former residents have slept silently. They rest in Kilpadder Famine Graveyard. These were the original people of Bridgie's road and the adjoining road that stretches from Kilpadder Cross to Collier's Quay. Houses at the time were small, one-roomed dwellings, built of stone and of mud kneaded with straw. Forty such houses, accompanied by tiny plots, stood along these two roads, and here too was the little church of St Peter. The area at the time was the property of the Frewen estate, who were the local landlords. Poverty was rife, and the mainstay food was the potato. When the potato crop failed in 1847, the famine came and people died of starvation. The Kilpadder road became known as 'Hell Street'. Famine pits were opened in Kilpadder, and the people were buried in them wearing the clothes in which they died. Many of those who survived emigrated on the coffin ships while others remained behind to contend with hunger and strife. It was a very black period in Irish history.

Time moved on, and Ireland recovered, and with the passage of decades nature reached out and reclaimed its own. The small field became shrouded in briars and buried in obscurity. Locals, however, never forgot those poor people, and local children were instructed to bless themselves when passing Kilpadder. One of these children was Mary Nolan, who, on her way to school walked past this overgrown hillside field every day. Her mother told her the story of the famine graveyard and of the need to acknowledge those forgotten souls. The story made a lasting impression on the mind of this sensitive child. She was never to forget Kilpadder Famine Graveyard and hoped that one day those people would be properly commemorated.

The mills of God grind slowly, but grind exceedingly well, and the bones of the ancestors in Kilpadder Famine Graveyard called out to be remembered. Then a descendant of a local person who had emigrated to America answered the call. Out of the blue came a query from a man whose ancestors were buried in Kilpadder: he wished to come and visit the burial place of his people.

By an amazing quirk of fate he made contact with Mary Nolan. Mary, now the well-known artist Mary Nolan O'Brien, had her work online, and, through this website, Bob Murphy of Boston, who was deeply interested in genealogy, made contact. He came to visit and expressed a wish that his ancestral graveyard be restored and made into a place of reverence and respect. He joined forces with fellow Bostonian Jim Calvey, and with the financial help of the Knights and Ladies of the St Finbarr Cork Club, New England, he got the project on the move.

For Mary, it was the answer to a prayer, and she engaged with the local community in getting things under way at home. The graveyard was situated on the land of a local farmer, who immediately gave permission for the restoration project. Then the old Irish *meitheal* method of the neighbours getting together for the job came into action. The site, under the careful guidance of an archaeologist from the local council, was carefully restored and fenced off. The little graveyard is on a steep hill, which necessitated a lot of careful grading and planting. Under the guidance of Mary, the forgotten graveyard was turned into wildflower garden surrounded by a hedge of native plants. Her husband, Joe, made a little wooden gate leading in off the road. A carefully chosen stone bears the name of the graveyard. While all this work was in progress, the local priest, Fr Finbarr Crowley, went to visit friends in a Boston parish where he often helped out, and by amazing coincidence this happened to be the parish of Bob and Jim! So further contacts were formed. It was decided that Mass would be celebrated in our famine graveyard on 24 July 2015. The Americans would come over for the occasion, and the locals would gather. After Mass and prayers, tea and cakes would be served, so that people would have time to meet the benefactors, reminisce and celebrate the blessing of the Kilpadder Famine Graveyard. An SOS went out for home-baking and prayers for fine weather. The baking was a surety, but the weather was up to divine providence. But hopefully the ancestors would intercede!

The summer of 2015 will not be remembered for its good weather, and Friday, 24 July was to prove no different. It dawned grey and misty, with intermittent showers. In case the showers proved persistent, Mary and her husband, who had already put a huge effort into the restoration, came with a large canopy which they placed over the altar that had been erected in the ruin of the tiny church at the foot of the hill. They placed another canopy over the eating area by the roadside. Mary hung lanterns containing candles off the trees, and rows of chairs were arranged on the grassy area around the altar. On the hill behind the altar the wildflowers glistened with raindrops, and that afternoon the only sound breaking the silence was the birds in the

adjoining Dromkeen Wood and the musical gurgle of the nearby stream. Stillness filled the air, and one felt that the residents of this long-abandoned graveyard were awaiting a sacred acknowledgement of their existence.

Then slowly the mist cleared and blue skies appeared between the overhanging trees. Cars purred up the narrow road and were directed into an adjoining field, and people coming through the gateway into the graveyard stopped to read the plaque telling its history. The rows of seats in front of the altar filled up with people, while groups stood at both ends. Parishioners and many others had come back to honour this special place on this historic occasion.

Absolute silence descended as Fr Finbarr began Mass, and one felt that the congregation was greater than those visibly present. It was an occasion laden with the presence of the past. The readings were done by the American visitors, descendants of those who had survived the coffin ships, and the Prayers of the Faithful were recited by local children, descendants of those who had survived at home. Hymns were sung and soft music played. It was the linking together of the many tangled strands of our chequered history and a reaching out of hands across the sea.

After Mass, Mary thanked everybody who had helped to make the occasion possible, especially Bob and Jim, who both told the gathering how happy they were to be present for this historic event. People gathered in groups to enjoy tea and home-made goodies and were glad of the opportunity to thank the Americans for their generosity of spirit.

As dusk gathered over Kilpadder, people began to leave and head back to the village. As they went out the gate, many looked back to view the little hillside graveyard, now covered in wildflowers, and felt pleased that they had been here at this special time. All went home glad that after over a hundred and fifty years the graves of Kilpadder had finally been blessed and the bones of the ancestors were at last resting in sacred ground.

A seat has been placed in this small hillside graveyard where you can sit quietly listening to birdsong from the surrounding wood and the stream gurgling beside you. You will not be alone here as the spirits of the past will be all around you because this is truly a sacred place.

Chapter 12

Back to Simplicity

In March, we had a mission in the parish. The timing was perfect. We had been through a long, wet, dreary winter, and, like the ground around us, we were battered, washed out and drained of the necessary nutrients to meet the challenges of spring and summer. We were in sore need of divine composting, spiritual sustenance and the bright sunny days that stimulate new growth. Then, miraculously, with the start of the mission, the rain cleared, and bright, sparkling spring sunshine dried up the sodden land and put pep back into our step. Long ago, the annual mission was a challenge, with grim reminders of doom for those who strayed from the 'one true path', but now it is usually seen as a kind of cleansing of the spirit and a fresh start for the times ahead. Like all good

planting projects, the necessary seeds had been sown back in autumn. The Parish Council had booked two missionaries to come in the spring. Missionaries, like garden planners, come in many guises. We were looking for people who would provide inspirational and visionary makeovers, not dull dudes who would stunt our growth. We cast our bread upon the waters and waited to see what the tide would bring in.

A month prior to the mission, a reconnaissance man arrived. This was Fr Brian, one of the two Redemptorist priests who were to give the mission. The Redemptorist order was once the ultimate 'hellfire and thunder brigade', delivering terrifying missions all over the country, but all that has changed and a new church is being born. Though still in the throes of excruciating labour pains, we are slowly seeing a new creation emerging. Both the laity and the clergy are still uncertain as to how this new baby will grow.

Our reconnaissance man was young, solid and open to our ideas and suggestions. It boded well for things to come. On one point, he was, however, adamant. In our parish, we actually have two churches, and this can sometimes lead to 'them and us' thinking. We had toyed with the idea of alternate nights. But Fr Kevin firmly advocated staying put in one church for the nightly mission as switching around would only lead to confusion. To balance things out between the two communities, we would have morning Mass in both churches, but at the different times. The nightly mission would be at 7.30 in the village church and Mass there at 7 in the morning. Rising at 6.30 every morning for a week would soften our cough for us! The other half of the parish could sleep on until 9.30am and would also host a healing Mass for the sick at a later time. That kept most of us half-happy!

Being a missionary in today's world requires a multitude of skills, as we were to discover throughout the week. The mission themes were left up to us as Fr Brian felt that we knew best the requirements of our parish. The overall theme, we decided, should be 'Welcome'. This decision had evolved from an encounter the previous week between our parish priest, Fr Finbarr, and an old parishioner, who, over the years, had lived the kind of life that he now regretted and came seeking comfort and solace. Fr Finbarr had comforted him as best he could and asked him if he would like to come back to church whenever he felt he could. But the man told him, 'No, I cannot come back. I am gone too long. I would not feel welcome.' That man set the main mission theme. The other themes we wanted to explore were healing, hope, forgiveness, family and community. Who would not want all of these in their lives?

The first challenge was to spread the word. The regular church-goers posed no problem as they would come anyway. They are the perennials. Constant and dependable, they pay their dues and keep the show on the road. But in our parish, as in every other, we have the annuals who come for special occasions, and then we have the rare plants that are fussy growers and can fade away but sometimes flower again. For the mission, we wanted to gather all these flowers for a shot of divine 'Miracle-Gro'. In the garden, this engenders amazing growth, so, as Sr Stan advises, the mission could be good gardening for the soul.

So we got little brochures printed. A lot of thought went into these. We were inspired by the painting in the Sistine Chapel, *The Creation of Adam* by Michelangelo, where God's finger reaches towards that of Adam. We came up with the image of a welcoming handshake for our brochure. The plan was to distribute one to each house in the parish.

A parish network is a great system. In our parish, we have over twenty 'station' areas, and each area is made up of a number of townlands. Each station area hosts an annual Mass attended by the neighbours, and the house hosting the Mass organises everything. So it was simply a case of getting a bundle of brochures to all the station areas from where they would be distributed. When we gathered on the night of the distribution, there happened to be choir practice on in the church and a perpetual adoration on in the prayer room, so all the usual suspects were readily available. Before the meeting was over, bundles of brochures were on their way to every house in the parish. To be sure that the word was out, we had large signs bearing the welcoming hands and the dates of events erected at strategic locations throughout the parish. The details also went on our Facebook page and Twitter. Changed times since Jesus was on the road! He sat in a boat or on the side of a mountain and they gathered. He had advised that having cast the bread upon the waters you then stood still, so we followed that advice.

On the Sunday preceding the start of the mission, Fr Brian came back to whet our appetites, and we discovered that he was into congregational singing and was no mean singer himself. That was a plus, as singing raises the spirits. On the opening night, the second of the two appeared. This was Fr Kevin, a Belfast man, who was older, leaner and funnier than Fr Brian. Then, as the week progressed, they both blossomed, and we discovered that these two guys were on the ball. On the first night, they told the young people that there would be a gift for any 7.30 Mass attender. How will this work, we wondered? But these two men had their homework done, and the following morning after Mass, the young people trooped up the aisle and glowed with delight when they each received a special wristband, which, apparently, is the in thing at the moment with the young. The next morning, the young crowd had doubled. Blackmail? Maybe, but harmless and it worked. They were both wonderful communicators and got their spiritual message across with wit and finesse. People enjoyed listening to them, and the crowd grew bigger as the week went on, particularly at early-morning

Mass which, curiously enough, had a huge appeal.

The week had some special moments, and one was on the night when the whole congregation was invited to stand and face west towards our school, which is across the road from the church, and raise our hands to bless our young. Then to face the back door of the church and bless the ancestors, who, down through the decades, had come through this door to pray: into my mind came Uncle Jacky, Aunty Peg, Gabriel, my cousin Con and my sister Ellen, who had all prayed here. I imagine that it was the same for everyone in the congregation, who all remembered their family members, many of whom are buried in the surrounding graveyard. Then we faced the altar and blessed the many priests who had served in our parish. It was symbolic and powerful.

The night on the theme of forgiveness got off to a great start with Fr Kevin retelling the Frank O'Connor story 'My First Confession', and, because he was a superb reader fit to read for *Book at Bedtime*, waves of laughter rippled around the congregation. The occasion was a reflection of the welcome transformation that we have seen in our church in recent times. Confession has been reborn as reconciliation. The terminology says it all. Some of us still remember the musty confessionals in which the priest peered out from behind bars like a jailer or dark curtains parted to reveal the face of judgement. All gone! Now we waltz around the church to the sound of soothing music.

We had an inspiring night on the meaning of community, and when we looked around the church, we realised that this is what it is all about. The sense of support and the togetherness with each other. I thought a lot about John Donne's poem:

No man is an island, entire of itself;
every man is a piece of the continent,
a part of the main.

Their final message of the mission to us was that the church of the pew was broadening out and being replaced by the church on the street.

On the last morning, outside the church door I met a young neighbour, who told me, 'I was dragged down to Mass!' 'By who?' I asked. 'By me,' her seven-year-old piped up, 'all the boys in school were going.' 'I'm sorry that I didn't come all week,' his mother told me as she surveyed the crowd around us. 'Everyone seems to be in great form.'

We have four schools in our parish, and later that day I met a young teacher from one of the outlying schools who told me with surprise, 'The main topic of conversation for my crowd during the week was the mission. They loved it.' We had hoped that the old-fashioned mission stalls would be there during the week because these children would have enjoyed them, but that medium of marketing must no

longer be popular. After the mission, the general consensus throughout the parish was that all who had attended felt better after the week.

I was yet to find out that God speaks in many voices because later that week a man who had not seen the inside of a church since his mother took him told me, 'That mission was very important for the young.' 'In what way?' I enquired. 'Well, in life, when the shit hits the fan, you need an anchor, and that will be there for them.' Then I ran into a book-loving friend who is not into church-going either, but when I enquired, 'What are you reading at the moment?' she answered, to my surprise, '*Conversations with God.*' 'With God?' I echoed. 'Yes, it was a *New York Times* best-seller.'

Undoubtedly, Jesus has got out of the boat and come down off the mountain.

Chapter 13

Buried in Books

Yesterday, as I went in the door of Waterstones', I prayed silently, 'Dear Lord let me see in here only books that are beyond temptation,' but God was not listening, and I came out with two. It is not that I do not enjoy buying books, but the problem is that I live in a house bursting with books. I did not create this situation all by myself, and it did not happen overnight. I was ably abetted and assisted by a husband who was into books on the Irish language, the magic power of the mind, sports and tomes on how to Do It Yourself. If you are into any of these pursuits, there is an endless supply of volumes available to feed your needs.

Over our many years together, I never took up a new hobby or cultivated an interest on which my beloved did

not have an informative book – or if not in stock one was soon acquired. He was also a great fan of joining book clubs, and there were queues of them offering temptation beyond resistance. I could paper the walls with DIY books, and I could carpet the floor with books on gardening. Simultaneously, he acquired leather-bound encyclopedias, which would require a strong pony to shift them, and as soon as the children could read and write they were similarly catered for.

Because the house was big and rambling, these books all sneaked in unobtrusively and onto shelves all over the house, from where they were occasionally lifted for consultation, but otherwise silently gathered dust. Books make comforting house companions that sit serenely on shelves smiling conspiratorially as they buddy up and make room for more and more friends to gather in around them.

To further exasperate the problem, a bookish cousin moved in and, with time, helped to fill adjoining rooms with more books. He was into science, history, beekeeping and antique books and frequently browsed through second-hand bookshops for first editions. Over the years, he even accumulated – and stored in meticulous order – ancient tattered copies of the Capuchin Annual journal.

Then, after decades of book-buying, these two bookworms moved up to the heavenly library, leaving behind them quantities of books that had to be seen to be believed – which leads one to the conclusion that one of the reasons that women generally outlive men is because the Almighty, in his all-knowing wisdom, knows that the women who remain will tidy up. (Though a smart son of mine thinks that the reason for the earlier male demise is that the Man Above leaves the ladies in the departure lounge until they are too old and tired to give him any trouble when they finally arrive at his pearly gate! That, of course, is mere male conjecture.)

However, my problem was not totally a male creation. My sister Ellen, who was into mind/body/spirit and the history of 1916 – she had a framed copy of the Proclamation at the foot of her bed – had gathered many books on both subjects. Also, for some years, we had a genteel lady of the Ascendancy in residence who was into Molly Keane books. Both were avid readers, and when they departed their books remained here too. Now it was just me and all these books. What to do?

There is a thing called Murphy's Law which declares that 'If it can happen it *will* happen and at the worst possible time,' and, true to form, before the book problem could be resolved the roof sprang a leak. To be honest, this did not come as a complete surprise as the old roof had been slightly incontinent for years. Now, however, the strategically placed aids for drips no longer worked and drastic surgery was required. And, as well, there were other jobs that had been pending for years, and, of course, now it was a case of 'while we are at it let's get that – and that, and that – done too.'

Getting in the builders is no small event, but when you

are undertaking major works it is a prospect of nerve-racking proportions. Before the builders entered the house, the books had to be cleared away. They occupied rooms through which the builders would be plodding with muddy boots and where they would be taking down partitions. So these old friends, who had spent years on shelves serenely smiling down at me, had to be whipped from their comfortable perches, all boxed up and temporarily stacked in territory that was not under builder attack.

They were packed into boxes with no consideration for class, creed or gender: PH Pearse was tucked in with Penelope Hobhouse, and weighty Samuel Levis with racy Jilly Cooper. As I surveyed the multitude of stacked boxes, I assured them and their departed owners that one day I would be back to rescue them and give them the select location that they all deserved.

The builders came and went, and I did not crack up completely, though at times it was touch and go. Eventually peace and quiet returned, and I no longer woke to the sound of hammers thumping off the roof. As is usual after a major house overhaul, it took time to adjust to the new regime and get the house back to working order. Gradually everything found its rightful place. The books alone remained to be sorted. They were on silent standby, quietly waiting for their day to come. Occasionally, when I ventured to look into the rooms of stacked boxes, I assured them, '*Tiocfaidh ár lá*.'

Because rearranging the books would be a job of marathon proportions requiring the right frame of mind, I put the sorting and shelving on the long finger again. Perhaps the motivating factor finally was the annoying fact that if I wanted to look something up or read a favourite poem, the books were all buried in boxes. It was simply no place to have books, especially books that had been friends for years. I was determined that at last there had to be a sorting job done and proper law and order introduced. Sometimes if you are aiming for perfection, the result is that you do nothing: you set the bar too high and the challenge deters you.

At last, one fine day, I got a rush of blood to the head. All of a sudden I had the mind on me to do it. The first requirement, as in building a house, was location; the second requirement was shelves, and lots of them, and the final requirement was a man to put up the shelves. In the course of the house overhaul, an art studio had come into being at one end of an upstairs corridor, and in it was a high blank wall. Ideal for bookshelves, I decided.

Next plan: introduce a son who is handy with a hammer to the said wall. Was it sound? he wondered. Was it concrete or stone? Would it hold brackets? Would the brackets hold the weight of the books? Could you drill it deep enough? Was it dry? The questions were endless. Men see problem! Women see solution! Eventually a meeting of minds came about due to the fact that I kept my mouth glued shut when

I really felt like opening it and braying like a donkey. Now, at times silence is golden. This was one of those times.

My handyman son was on night shift at work so he gave me long and detailed instructions on what to order. A slight problem arose: the world had moved on to centimetres and metres, but Alice was still in feet and inches. But with the help of a tolerant young shop assistant, who must have a confused granny at home, I concluded, we got it all figured out. The plan was wide shelves at the bottom to carry the heavyweights so that if a sudden collapse did occur I would not be rendered lifeless beneath them, and the higher we went the slimmer the volumes would get.

Dozens of shelves of varying width and length, with a variety of brackets, accompanied by long, steel strips into which they would lock, were delivered. All ready for action. Gone are the days when my father would simply arrive home from the creamery with his pockets full of screws and nails and long timber boards swaying across the creamery cart to be borne upstairs by that impatient carpenter, girded with a hammer, saw, ruler – and a short fuse. The onerous job would then begin of creating holes in stubborn old stone walls that had a mind of their own on how deeply they would allow penetration. Sometimes he had to resort to driving solid planks of wood into these cavernous walls with the butt end of a hatchet to provide shelf supports. As this work progressed, a deep well of annoyance began to open up in the carpenter. This shot into eruption in spasmodic outbursts of unimaginable language capable of igniting the surrounding timber work. Every saint in heaven was called on, and not in the most flattering of appeals, and even God himself was not beyond mention. The unfortunate board that was a few inches short when cut with a bow saw became 'a whore' of indescribable lineage. While all this was in progress, his cap slid to the back of his head, with beads of perspiration gathering on his forehead, and his tongue swept across his mouth like a demented windscreen wiper. His daughters danced around him, anticipating his every need. Fast reaction was the name of the game, otherwise you could be the target of a flying ruler.

In total contrast, his grandson, who is called after him, requested my immediate departure from the room so that he could work in silence and avoid the views of his opinionated mother. When I chanced a silent peep, my gaze was met by long, laminated, steel strips running up the wall from floor to ceiling. Penetrative drills and electric screwdrivers were whirring in action – a far cry from the butt end of a hatchet and the timber planks of his grandfather. If there was a slight hitch in proceedings, all I would hear was the repetition of the one word which now seems to be the only word in our modern world that serves as release of frustration. No colourful stream of heavenly bodies or tirades of unseemly whores were called on board.

Eventually all was accomplished, and I had an array of shelves fit for the National Library. There were no librarians or archivists, however, to effect a proper layout or indexing system. Just me and boxes of books. And boxes of books are heavy beyond belief so further male muscle had to be coaxed and blackmailed into dragging them from all over the house to their final resting place on this floor.

Then began the long sort. It went on for weeks because big decisions had to be made about what to keep and what to let go to the charity shops. This led to hours of browsing and the discovery of old letters and photographs once used as bookmarks. And hours spent sitting on the floor led to the unpleasant discovery that my ability for fast rising was seriously impaired. I regretted my abandonment of yoga. Then I wised up and introduced into the scene a comfortable old rocking chair, which had the added bonus of tilting forward to assist upward mobility. This chair had been rescued from a junk shop and lovingly restored, and now paid back in full for the investment.

Eventually I got to the point where the books were ready for shelving. The plan was to introduce some sort of system which would eliminate hours of searching to find what you were looking for. This led to endless hours of placing and then increasing the allowed space when a lost companion of those already shelved appeared. Gradually some sort of organisation of categories began to emerge. I could not say that I succeeded one hundred percent in creating the perfect system, but at least now there is some law and order to the entire collection and you might find what you were looking for in minutes rather than hours.

When the floor was cleared and all the shelves full, the books smiled down at me, and my sense of satisfaction was immense. I think that the late owners were smiling too. Our books are so much part of who we are, and now I sometimes sit on the rocking chair with the sun streaming in the south-facing window, overlooking Dromkeen Wood, and take down one of the books and enjoy a leisurely browse. I am very grateful to the enlightened book-lovers with whom I have shared this house.

Chapter 14

The Impossible Dream

'We'll need to be in Beara before dark on Friday evening,' I told my daughter. 'But why?' she asked in an amused tone of voice. 'Don't you know that I have lights on my car?' 'Lights or no lights,' I told her firmly, 'that road from Castletownbere to Allihies is lofty terrain, not to mention when we leave the main road to manoeuvre down the steep incline to the centre. And if there's black ice, which is quite possible at this time of year, we could go waltzing down that slippery slope to eternity. I have no ambition to end my days as fish food in Bantry Bay.' 'Not to worry,' she told me airily, 'we'll be there before dark.'

This trip to the Dzogchen Beara centre had been on my bucket list for a long time. I've always been fascinated by the lifestyle of the Poor Clare contemplative nuns and curious to know what enabled them to survive that existence of silence and continuous prayer. Then, on visiting Skellig Michael, a tiny remote rocky island off the Kerry coast, the thought of the monks surviving out there in stone beehive huts, enduring all kinds of weather in that beautiful but barren place, brought the same thought to mind. How did people survive in these places? What was the secret? The only common denominator that I could discern between the enclosed order of the Poor Clare nuns and the Skellig monks was meditation. Could that possibly be the key?

But ordinary living distracted me from my quest for more insight and information, and I got bogged down with rearing children and running a business. It was many years later before I found my way back to this voyage of discovery. Here in our parish of Innishannon, the Rosminian order has a monastery where they care for adults with special needs, and they also have another house in Glencomeragh, County Waterford, which is in a beautiful valley at the foot of Slieve na mBan. When I was young, one of my father's favourite songs was 'Slieve na mBan', and, because he did not have a musical ear, he chanted rather than sang it, but his chant enhanced rather than diminished the beauty of the melody. So when a friend invited me to join her for a contemplative weekend at the foot of Slieve na mBan, I jumped at the chance to get away from balance sheets that refused to balance and teenagers jumping with uncontrollable hormones. A weekend in a silent valley away from it all seemed like a dream come true.

The weekend was guided by an inspirational young Jesuit who obviously savoured the peace of meditation. He told us that the mind was like a tree full of jumping monkeys and the only way to quieten them was to quieten ourselves – not scream louder than the monkeys! That meditation weekend washed out my cluttered mind and undid the knots along the tops of my shoulders, and I went home viewing the world through calmer eyes. Unfortunately, the new-found tranquillity did not last. I endeavoured to keep up the daily meditation practice, knowing that it was the key to serenity, but soon the demands of everyday living pushed the meditation time aside, and it became a hit-and-miss event. I was to discover that meditation, though simple, is not easy. There must be an element in us humans that even though we know that something is good for us we still allow it to be pushed aside by more demanding events.

My next encounter with the practice was when a calm, serene nun of the order of St Thérèse of the Child Jesus came to work with the Rosminians in our parish, and she was into meditation. She invited some of us to join her, and she suggested a weekly group meeting. In my ignorance, I thought that this did not make sense as I had considered meditation to be something that you did on your own. How wrong you can be! The weekly group meeting keeps you in touch and even if more demanding activities shove the daily meditation sideways, at least once a week you came back to your centre, a bit like a slimming and exercise meeting. It brought me back on track.

A few years later, on a beautiful June day, two friends invited me to travel over the Beara Peninsula. As we climbed the high mountainy road from Castletownbere to Allihies, we saw a blue sign saying Dzogchen Beara. It pointed across the clifftop, and we turned in that direction. We seemed to be going over the edge of the world. Soon, gorgeous billowing banners fluttering along the hedgerows like Swiss Guards led us down the steep side of the mountain. We arrived onto a ledge, and there, perched on the very tip of the precipice, was what looked like a tiny oratory clinging to the side of the rocks. To reach it, we climbed up wooden steps and into an open porch. A scattered collection of shoes conveyed the message of bare feet, so we removed our shoes. There was about the whole place a sense of quietness and peace, so without consciously thinking about it we fell silent.

Nothing could prepare you for the breathtaking experience of entering that room. The sea and the sun simply swam in over you. There was nothing between you and the sea but glass, and you were dazzled by daylight. The few people in the room were either sitting motionless or kneeling on the floor. We quietly joined them. Finally we had to drag ourselves away to continue our journey. I knew that one day I would come back to this amazing place in the mountains.

And now I was on my way, and I had not instigated the journey. To my surprise, it was my daughter, who works in the IT business in the city, who suggested coming here. 'How did you hear of this place?' I enquired. 'Two of the lads at work were there last year and loved it,' she told me. I was pretty amazed that in that high-tech company of sharp-brained young blades there were individuals who had discovered and wanted to investigate this world of calmness and contemplation. And when we arrived there, I was further surprised to find that many of the almost forty participants were young males.

Dusk was coming down over the Beara Peninsula as we crawled carefully down the steep, narrow incline into the Dzogchen Centre. 'We are not in Kansas anymore, Toto,' my daughter quipped. I kept my fingers crossed in case an approaching car appeared as there was no way two cars could get by on this little road.

After a light supper, we gathered in the Shrine Room. I was back in the room of dazzling daylight, only now the dark sea sighed all around the glass walls. Tall, softly spoken Andrew and a gentle-faced woman named Susan were the facilitators. That session was the format for all the others that

followed over the weekend. Andrew and Susan took turns at guiding us into stillness and introduced us to the different steps of meditation. Then they turned on a central screen, and a Buddhist monk revealed simple truths of the paths to inner serenity. Now and then we gathered in small groups for discussion, and afterwards were again stilled into restful meditation. It was a calming, settling experience.

In between sessions, my daughter and I climbed the steep path to our accommodation in the Healing Centre. During the day the sea shimmered all around us, and late at night the trees and bushes glistened with frost and a huge moon looked at itself in the navy-blue sea. Each morning we woke to the arrival of the sun over the horizon when it poured streams of rainbow colours across the bay. It is a mesmeric landscape.

Everything, including eating, took place in the Shrine Room, where we collected our vegetarian food in trays off a corner table and sat around the floor or on chairs quietly chatting or silently looking out to sea. After one session, I found myself sitting beside an athletic young man, who, as soon as we began to talk, I knew was American, and he told me that he had come especially for this retreat and that it was his first visit to Ireland. 'I had heard Ireland was beautiful,' he told me in awe, 'but this' – he waved his hand out towards the mountains and sea – 'is truly amazing.' I resisted the temptation to tell him that this was as good as it got!

Before leaving after lunch on Sunday, I picked up a book, *Dazzled by Daylight*, written in 2014 by Peter Cornish, who, in 1972, had what seemed like an impossible dream. He and his young wife had come across from England on the *Innisfallen* boat and taken the road into West Cork. They were dazzled by the beauty of the landscape. Their dream was to set up this centre, and, despite impossible odds, they kept going until it became a reality. They spent many nights in a doorless and windowless cottage when water flowed down the mountain in the back door and out the front; they struggled for years against the elements and the dangers of building on these dizzying heights above the sea. Finally, after years of struggling against the odds, the dream was realised. The Dzogchen Beara centre was created on tip of the Beara Peninsula in the depths of West Cork and now awaits all comers. It is for people of all religions and none. It is a beacon of light erected by a young couple who had what seemed like an impossible dream.

Chapter 15

Friendship

When we have a job to be done in the village that demands heavy machinery, my farmer friend and neighbour, Paddy, who can turn a tractor in very tight corners, always comes to the rescue. Over the years, he sometimes mentioned a friend of his called Donal, who lived in Dublin, and I assumed Donal to be around Paddy's age. Then, a few years ago, we were restoring our church and we had a craft fair to raise funds, and Donal came to help, bringing his handcrafted bowls and lamps, and I was surprised to discover that Donal was about twenty years older than Paddy and in a wheelchair. I was a bit intrigued by this and inquired as to how they had become friends.

It had all begun years earlier, when Paddy's father, then

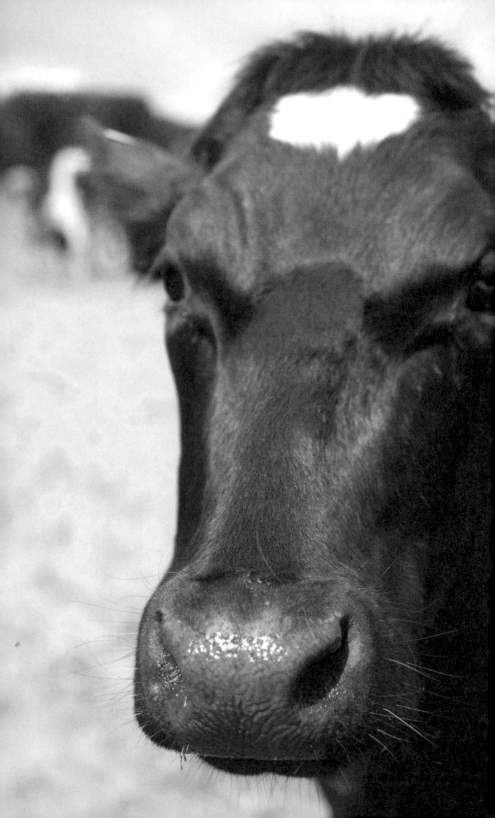

in his forties, was in hospital recovering from back surgery. Sharing the ward was a young man in his twenties, suffering from the after-effects of polio. The decades of age difference between the two men was bridged by the common bond of pain and suffering. A deep friendship grew between Paddy's father, a middle-aged farmer, and the younger Donal, a shipwright from a fishing village in the depths of West Cork. Confined to hospital for many months, they forged a deep understanding of each other's personality, and, during the tedious pain-filled nights, when neither could sleep, they kept each other sane.

Eventually, both men were sufficiently recovered to be discharged, and, though intending to keep in contact, they soon got caught up in their own lives and lost touch completely. Life was just too busy. During the following years, Paddy often heard his father and mother talk about Donal, and he became familiar with the name. Over the years, he came to realise that this special friend of his father's, whom he had never known, would never be forgotten by his parents, who would be forever grateful to this kind young man who had helped them through a tough patch of their lives.

Meanwhile, Donal left home and went to work in Dublin, where he married and raised a family, occasionally coming back home to visit his West Cork roots. Sometimes, when travelling through Innishannon, he thought of his old friend and wondered how he was getting on. But with a carful of children and not being sure of the correct address, he never quite got around to looking up his friend. Life was just too busy. Time went by, and then fate stepped in and played a hand. A niece of Donal's wife was in college with a girl from Innishannon, and one weekend while she was staying with her friend in Innishannon there was a wake at a neighbour's house. Back in Dublin, she happened to mention the wake to her mother, who in turn mentioned it to Donal. This triggered off memories in Donal. After a few pertinent questions he figured out that the man who had died could be his old friend. A sense of regret for the many years without being in touch came over Donal. He decided that the next time he was passing through the village he would try and make contact. His friend might be gone, but Donal felt the need to meet his family, to see his home place and remember him. Death can sometimes propel us into taking steps that might have been at the back of our minds for a long time. He realised that his friend's children would now be grown men with the same age gap between him and them as had been between himself and their father when they first met in hospital.

Some months later, when he was driving through Innishannon, Donal stopped and made a few enquiries. He found himself on the road to the farm. When he drove into the yard, there was a man leading a horse towards him. Doing mental arithmetic on the years, Donal concluded that this could be the youngest of the family – who had probably never even heard of him. This man would wonder what had brought him. Still, Donal wound down the window and asked hesitantly, 'Did your father die recently?' That's right,' Paddy answered, puzzled. 'I knew him many years ago when he was your age,' Donal told him. 'But you've probably never heard of me. My name is Donal Brown.'

'Oh, I know who you are,' Paddy assured him in delighted surprise, holding out his hand in welcome. 'Long ago, you were in hospital with my father. He never forgot you, and over the years my mother and himself often talked of you. I felt that I knew you too. Come in! It's great to meet you after all these years.'

Donal was greatly relieved to be so warmly welcomed to the home of the man who had been so kind to him all those years before. Many hours later, after a long conversation, Donal left, delighted that he had taken the time to call. It was as if the years had rolled back. The stitches of the relationship that had been put on hold had been picked up and the deep bond of friendship between him and this family rekindled. It was a good feeling.

After that, Donal became a regular caller on his way to West Cork, and Paddy and his family visited him and his family in Dublin. The friendship that had begun between the two men of different generations many years previously blossomed again between these two men of again different

generations. Over the years, the friendship enriched both their lives.

Due to his earlier brush with polio, Donal was eventually confined to a wheelchair, but this did not diminish his zest for life. He took up woodturning, a skill to which he introduced Paddy, and they both hugely enjoyed the shared hobby. Over the years, Paddy often talked of Donal and his skill as a wood turner, and when Paddy became similarly skilled, his products were much appreciated for our local fund-raisers.

Earlier this year, Donal died peacefully in his home, and Paddy travelled to Dublin to say goodbye to this friend whose friendship, as a young man, had enriched his father's life and years later as an old man had enriched his.

In memory of   Jer Desmond
1916 –   – 1999

And the
WORD
was made
FLESH
and
dwelt
Among us
St John
Chapter 1
Verse 14

Chapter 16

The Blue
Fountain Pen

I t was a most unusual wedding present. An elegant royal-blue fountain pen, resting amidst folds of soft satin in a matching blue leather case. It came from one of Gabriel's best friends, and we treasured it. Even though I cannot now remember what some of our other friends gave us, I can still see the blue fountain pen clearly. Back then I was too young and inexperienced to fully appreciate the depth of thought behind this beautiful gift, and somewhere along the road of living it got lost. Now I regret that. As I am a collector and hoarder, this is unforgivable. But that gift from a man who marched to the sound of his own drum is one of my most precious memories. Whenever I think of him and his pen, it brings a smile to my face and a ray of sunshine into my heart. He was born with a soul full of romance, and the practicalities of life never bothered him.

He called himself The Twin and his twin brother The Other Fella. The Other Fella emigrated early in life, and so The Twin was left to his own devices to run the family farm. It was the ideal situation for him. The farm consisted of top-quality land and was located on the edge of our village overlooking the river valley and Dromkeen Wood. It had breathtaking views which The Twin thoroughly enjoyed, and because the land was good he lived comfortable off it with very little effort on his part.

When he won a piano in a Sunday newspaper competition, he gave up farming completely and concentrated on teaching himself to play the instrument. He was already a superb violinist, and the piano put the icing on the cake of his musical delights. He derived huge enjoyment from his win. Callers to his house might be given a recital if the humour was on him, and I remember one Christmas Day when I was out for a walk with Gabriel, we dropped in and were treated to a wonderful impromptu concert. He was a free spirit, always doing exactly as he pleased.

The Twin loved women and always dreamed of finding the perfect partner, but none of his many romances ever blossomed as far as the altar rails. His dream in life was of the ideal romance. Maybe the fact that he was drawn to strong-willed, managerial women who wanted to control him had something to do with his lack of success. Some of his girlfriends saw The Twin as the perfect partner – but only if he could be moulded into a different model! And that was the rock on which all his romances floundered. The Twin was not for remoulding, and in the end his many girlfriends gave up the effort in frustration. He was like an elusive butterfly who could never be netted, and what he really needed was a creative dreamer who understood him and let him fly free. But he never once looked in that direction.

Music, singing, dancing and writing were the joys of his life, and he was part of everything that happened around the village. He made a huge contribution, not only to village life but also to the recording of the history of Innishannon. If something caught his fancy, he put pen to paper and wrote verses about it. Quick-witted and eloquent, he viewed life as a game not to be taken too seriously. He eulogised his girlfriends in verse and thought nothing of converting a poem into a song and giving a rendition at a local concert, much to the enjoyment of the audience but to the great annoyance and embarrassment of the current girlfriend. Afterwards, he was surprised when he got a sharp dismissal. He attempted to teach one long-term girlfriend to drive his car. But this had unhappy consequences, and thereafter he penned a poem about the undertaking. To the The Twin, everything was a story.

In twelve months of courting
She never came late
But bright as a bird
She was down at the gate,
We drove to Kinsale
And she viewed with delight
Where O'Neill and O'Donnell
Were beat in the fight.
But not long after that
We too were at war
When she asked me politely
To teach her the car.
But I had no patience
And she had great skill
I was told by the lassie
From the top of Camp Hill.
We had many scrapes
And we had many spills
But were still on track
Till down by Jagoe's Mills
As she tore at the gears
I gave a wee shout
And knew by her face
That 'twas all up the spout.

That was the end of that romance!

But with parish happenings The Twin was on much safer ground, and it is here that his strongest contributions to the community were made. As our parish hall was being built by voluntary labour, he put pen to paper to record it all as the building took place. On the night of the opening, he recited the following on stage, much to the delight of the audience, most of whom had been involved in the entire process. Even when you don't know the people involved, you can get a real sense of local history in the making.

The Parish Hall

As we meet here tonight we are thrilled with delight
In opening this beautiful hall
Well 'tis only true that 'twas long overdue
But we hadn't a chew that was all.
Then some fortunate gale blew up from Kinsale
Father Riordan to hail as a friend
He could cut out red tape and put things in shape
We were soon on a great upward trend.

Among things great and small he got at the dance hall
And we knew he was on the right track
He said, 'Boys all be here, bring your sledges and gear
And we'll start to pull down the old shack.'
Well the work did proceed at incredible speed

A fresh team each night was the plan
Gabriel would appear like a head engineer
And made Connors a permanent man.

Excavation took place for a sound solid base
And McCarthy's bulldozer did bark
Then after excavation we put down the foundation
And worked every night until dark.
Soon the structure took shape true to plumb rule and tape
All things working according to plan.
And if stuck in a pinch we could look to Joe Lynch
That able and qualified man.

We had one powerful factor, Jerry Crowley, contractor,
He had erected from sheds to lounge bars
And the masoning by Maddens, a sad heart would gladden
Sure for long years the Maddens were stars
And our cross-country runner McCarthy from Skeough
Put into it all he possessed
In tradesmanship, skill and a little know-how
To have him we really were blessed.

All the names of the men can't come under my pen
Whom our head engineer did employ
But O'Halloran hauled up the bricks like a horse
And Tom Collins we all did enjoy.

I can't miss Michael Ryan, a dear friend of mine,
All the lighting design here he planned
An electrical genius, his lights shine like Venus
You'd think you were in Fairyland.

The ladies gave much, 'twas the last final touch
They swept and they scrubbed it each night
They painted and polished from bottom to top
'Till they had it all sparkling and bright.
So with every help-out, from within and without,
It flowered like a fine work of art
From the smooth maple floor to the brick by the door
It would cheer up the loneliest heart.

Now the hall is complete, it is noble and neat
'Tis the pride of the village so grand
From Cork to Dungannon, no place like Innishannon
The loveliest spot in the land.
By the hall you could dream amid woodland and stream
And the beautiful bridge of renown.
You've the garage by Phil at the foot of the hill
And the Parson above looking down.

At the time, across the road from the hall a man called Phil ran a garage and the Church of Ireland rectory up the hill beside it had a resident clergyman.

Every parish and village needs a Twin to make its history by recounting all the small, local details. In his writings, The Twin recorded the social history of our parish, but many of his writings simply finished up inside in his head because once written he gave them away and never kept copies. Many got lost. When we began to publish our Christmas magazine, *Candlelight*, we rounded him up every year and got him to write down one of his stories or poems. At least we now have those for posterity. People can also enjoy the stained-glass window of the monk in the scriptorium that his two nieces had installed in our church in his honour.

After he had read my first book, *To School through the Fields*, The Twin called to see me. He always spoke in a soft, whispering voice, as if he was confiding the most profound secret to his listeners. 'You know, Alice,' he whispered, 'as I read your book I said to myself, she is getting it right. But will she remember the hawk? If she does not have the hawk she will not get it right. And then I came to the hawk. You forgot nothing.' I knew exactly what he meant: the children of my childhood years spent a lot of time guarding the chickens from the hawk, and if I'd left that out he'd have felt that an essential part of the story of those days was missing. But it was there! It was a most unusual book review. He was always into the heart of the matter as he saw it. No newspaper book reviewer would approach a book from The Twin's angle. Then, just as he was about to leave, he surprised me by asking, 'Alice, do you remember the blue fountain pen?' 'It's long gone,' I told him regretfully. 'Giving me that at the time, you really were casting pearls before swine.' 'Never mind,' he whispered gently, 'it did its job.' Before I could process this statement, he put his hand on my shoulder and told me quietly, 'You can do a lot for Innishannon now.'

I think he felt that he was handing on the torch.

Chapter 17

Watch Your Step!

A large, bouncing black dog led by a smiling, curly-haired young man ran down the hill onto the village street. In one hand was the dog lead and in the other a strange object. Could it possibly be … ? It looked like one! It *had* to be. Yes, it was a pooper scooper! A rare sight on our village street, or on the street of any Irish town or village. The sight brought a few of us to a standstill. We were stunned. This phenomenon warranted further investigation. The man was a newcomer to the village. He had to be interviewed. It is one of the pluses of village living that you can freely chat up a total stranger on the street.

'You are like manna in the desert,' one woman told him in an awestruck voice. 'Why?' he laughed. 'You're carrying

a pooper scooper,' she gasped. 'I would never bring my dog out without it,' he told her. 'Do you think you could introduce that practice here?' she implored. 'Are they that rare in the village?' he asked. 'Like gold nuggets,' she told him. 'Are you here long?' 'Just moved in,' he said. 'We were living in America for the last couple of years. If your dog pooed on the street over there, you would not dare walk away from it, people would absolutely not let you get away with it. As soon as your dog began to poo, people stood with pointing fingers demanding that you remove it immediately. And as well as that, it's against the law.'

'It's against the law here as well,' she told him, 'but nobody takes a blind bit of notice.' 'But what happens to the poo?' he asked curiously. 'We walk into it and curse the dog,' he was informed. 'But that doesn't make any sense,' he protested. 'Welcome home,' she smiled.

There are smelly unmentionables along the streets of most towns and villages in the country. They are deposited unceremoniously by our four-legged friends while their owners feel quite entitled to stand idly by as their dog does what a dog has to do. We passers-by do not have the moral courage, as they do in other countries, to insist on responsible dog-owner action. So the deposit remains, and we tut-tut over it and walk around it until a child or unwary adult comes along and sinks their shoe in it. Then it gets smeared along the pavement and eventually, after many shoes bear it away, it gets eroded out of recognition. Sounds disgusting. It is!

There is a law, but in reality it is not worth a pile of poo. In the case of dog poo, the best law-enforcers are us, the public. We did it with the smoking ban. But do we consider that tackling the problem of dog poo is beneath our dignity? As long as we think that, it will remain beneath our feet.

In our village, we have a new raised walk around The Bleach, and it was a wonderful facility for dog-owners, who were requested to keep their dogs on leads and to clean up after them where necessary. Young people play games here, so for health-and-safety reasons it was unacceptable to have dog poo on the grass. Neither request was observed, and now dogs are not allowed there. So the responsible dog-owners are suffering for the offences of the irresponsible ones.

Then we have the ownerless dog – there is always one in every village. A bit like the riderless horse in the Grand National, they create havoc. Now, while the jockey will come back to claim his horse, the dog-owner never appears. He just opens the door and lets the dog out to roam free and lets him back in again. In our village the main offender is a large, overweight mongrel with proportional production rates, who has free-range rambling privileges. Half-blind and half-deaf, and with limited mobility, he nevertheless negotiates his way safely across our extremely busy main road to the other side of the street, thus maintaining equal distribution of his favours all around.

So what is to be done with our doggy-poo problem? There seems to be no solution. Some Tidy Towns committee people keep a dustpan and brush especially for taking up other people's dog's poo off our street.

Come early summer, in villages and towns all around Ireland, teams of willing workers come out of hibernation. These are the Tidy Towns diehards! They plant, brush, paint and pick litter. All for the love of their own place. And of all the pursuits that the Tidy Towners take on board, poo removal and litter-picking are probably the most challenging. When litter-picking, you need to turn off your thinking facilities or you could finish up with a very low opinion of your fellow human beings: if you can think beautiful thoughts while you pick up other people's litter, you have definitely scaled the peak of a mental mountain. And if you can pick up the poo of someone else's canine delight without thinking bad thoughts about the owner, who stood witlessly aside while their four-legged friend did the needful, you are definitely in the halo brigade.

Being a Tidy Towner is a special calling, and all over Ireland people continue to answer that call. In Innishannon, we are no different. Tidy Towns is about gaining points in the competition, but more than that it is about love of your own place. Over the years, you work to beautify your home place, and, in the process, you make great friends and have a lot of fun. Still, the dog poo continues to be a smelly problem!

Chapter 18

Away with the Fairies

This year, a settlement of fairies moved into Drom-keen Wood. Last year, with grant-aided funding, this wood was revamped by the Tidy Towns committee. New walkways, steps and rails opened up the overgrown paths. People were delighted, and they poured in and enjoyed this haven of ancient trees, mossy slopes and the occasional glimpse of a rare red squirrel. People met and chatted on the pathways. There is something about a wood that encourages conversation.

The fairies heard about it and decided that this beautiful place could have possibilities for them. Could they set up a Dromkeen Fairyland? They sent in their surveyors, who came back with very positive reports. They reported back

that this wood was beautifully situated on a sloping hillside overlooking the Bandon river valley and the village of Innishannon. Perfect for a new fairyland!

But a wise old fairy cautioned that they should move with care and advised that first they should send a reconnaisance party to test the ground. They sent the most astute and demanding of the fairies to pick out the most ancient and safest trees. When they had selected their fairy homes, they sent out an SOS to the locals that they needed fairy doors. After all, who could live in a doorless house?

So the Innishannon Tidy Town group came to the rescue and asked a skilled local carpenter to create the doors. Jimmy McCarthy crafted tiny Gothic doors fit for a fairy house, and Tidy Towners, helped by the FÁS workers, painted them bright fairy-like colours and took them to the wood. You would imagine that placing fairy doors on the trees along paths in the wood would be a straightforward job. Not so! Fairies are not like us, and you need to get into their mindset to get things right. So to be sure to be sure that we would get the doors properly located throughout the wood where the fairies would like them, we decided to simply place the doors but not secure them in position until we had them all laid out along the paths. Some we hid behind trees, others were buried deep in tree recesses. This took time. We had started at around 10am, and by lunchtime we were still pacing the paths. Finally, all was to our satisfaction, and we began securing them into position. Then we decided to furnish them with mossy paths and to lay little stone walls around the houses. I admit I got carried away – and one of the FÁS lads declared that he was starving and headed for home, but the other lad was enjoying the make-believe. I think we had both slipped back into childhood mode.

Earlier in the year, a large tree had fallen and had been cut into logs. These we dragged up a steep path into a little lay-by between the trees to create a fairy meeting place. But when all were in position, it still lacked a fairy table, and we looked around the wood. Behind the little meeting place was a raised bank and out of it protruded a large, flat rock. Now, was this protruding rock a huge stone that could be shifted or was it part of a rock formation that went deep into the earth and was immovable? Only one way to find out! My willing helper dug around the edges, and we tried to shift it, but it would not be moved. Then, walking along the wood, came a tall, strong man, who saw our plight and came to the rescue: this was Oisín coming astride the horse. With two mighty tugs he established that it was indeed movable, and then rolled it down the bank, where it fell into position at the centre of the logs. The fairies had a gathering place.

As well as the fairy doors, we had also brought to the wood a strange-looking home-made mirror, retrieved from a dump. It was framed with twigs and looked exactly like what fairies might use. This necessitated Tarzan-like activity

to hang it high off a tree below one of the paths where the fairies, and children, could look across and see themselves. All finally done, we were delighted with ourselves, but when we emerged from the wood we realised we too were starving.

The fairies were thrilled. So much so that they sent messages to the Fairy Queen to move the whole kingdom to Dromkeen. And so it came to pass that the entire tizzy of fairies moved into Dromkeen Wood. In the lay-by, they set up their fairy village, with the large stone as the council table and the logs for seats. There they gather every night to dine and celebrate until the dawn breaks. So at night Dromkeen Wood belongs to the fairies! Now the fairies have a settlement of about twenty houses in Dromkeen. All you can see is their doors as you walk along the paths. But they are watching you! Did you know that fairies like to look beautiful? They use their large mirror, and when you look into it sometimes the fairies are looking over your shoulder. So visit the fairies in Dromkeen Wood and remember that the fairies like to keep their wood very, very clean.

Very late one night, last Christmas, a man driving past the wood saw fairy lights sparkling on a tree. He spread the word, and over the following weeks people went to see if it was true. And indeed it was. The fairies had put up their own fairy lights in the wood for Christmas.

Chapter 19

Rights of Way

Rights of way have always been a bone of contention in Ireland. We have an obsession with landownership, even tiny strips or muddy gaps, and neighbours have hounded each other through courts and spent fortunes on legal fees to be able to say, 'Keep out, this is mine.' Does it all go back to being invaded and having our land taken off us? Due to its accessibility and scenic siting, Innishannon has always been a sought-after location – even back in the ninth century it enticed the marauding Vikings to set their hats in our direction and sail their longships up the river. Sometimes now as I stand on the bridge at the western end of the village and look down the Bandon river, it is easy to imagine those longships. A romantic image, I know, but I'm glad

I live in these times rather than back then when warring between tribes was the name of the game and if they were not battling with each other they were fighting off invaders. If the invaders succeeded in gaining a foothold, they doled out land, which they now considered to be theirs, to their warring generals, who uprooted the former residents and planted in their own people. This did not lead to very cordial relations between the newcomers and the natives. This was how Innishannon was gifted by Oliver Cromwell to Thomas Adderley, whose family remained landlords here for a few generations.

Is it as a result of this history that it is so annoying when a new buyer moves in and blocks off a right of way? Rights of way can give a sense of continuity to a place in the midst of ever-changing ownership. A few years back, a right of way just outside the village was blocked off, but the fishermen who had always used it simply ignored the barrier and continued merrily on their usual route to the river. When the owner persisted, unflattering nicknames were painted on the road outside his gate. Nobody ever knew who did it, but the probability was that it was not actually the fishermen but some local bystander who was enjoying the battle of wits and wanted to add fuel to fire.

While individuals may fight to maintain a right of way, it is far more difficult for a community to do so. Here in the village we have had three rights of way which for many years gave the village access to the river. Now we have none; they have all been closed off by people who have ignored history and the rights of the village. It is very difficult for a voluntary organisation to sort out these situations as the only way to enforce the law is by the law, and that is a slippery slope that could divide a community. The Council does not want to know, and I suppose it is hard to blame them.

Around The Bleach, we now have a river walk which is in constant use because of the huge increase in traffic through the village. The Council have a long-term plan to extend this walk down along the river bank, but when that happens, if it does, there will be no village access to it because of the blocked rights of way. These access points would make the walk a much safer place, and the walk would be of far greater benefit to the people of the village, but the blockages will damage the pleasurable living and well-being of those who will come after us.

We do have one success story regarding rights of way. Between two roads at the edge of the village is an old link lane that became surplus to requirements when wider main roads were built. For a while, it remained in occasional use by adjoining farmers and as a short cut. Along the lane were the ruins of an old house which belonged to a man called Con, so it was known as Con's Lane. While roads were still quiet enough for walking, Con's Lane was not much used, but with the huge increase of traffic in recent years we in the

Tidy Towns committee thought of the idea of working on Con's Lane and turning it into a safe walking area.

Then a newcomer who had acquired an adjoining farm endeavoured to transform many fields into one field and in the process dumped all the displaced ditches into Con's Lane. It was blocked with stones, tree trunks and mounds of earth, and was totally impassable. What to do? We approached the culprit, and, after diplomatic negotiations, it was agreed that the blockage would be removed when his harvest was done and his fields were clear for machinery to come in and do the work. Eventually all was accomplished, and the lane was cleared. It is not the M50, but a rough, rocky lane, which makes one aware of the roads with which our ancestors had to be satisfied.

Then last October, on a sunny Saturday afternoon, a *meitheal* gathered with bags of daffodil bulbs and assorted wildflowers, and we planted them along both sides of the lane. Planting complete, we gathered on the green area outside the ruin of Con's house and had tea, apple cake and currant cake. Hopefully, in years to come, Con's Lane will glow with wildflowers that will sprout up along the ditches, and the wild ferns will come back to reclaim what was rightfully theirs.

Chapter 20

Planting History

When, as a child, I first read the story 'Eoinín na nÉan', I fell in love with its author, Pádraig Pearse. That autumn, long ago, as I watched the swallows line up for departure, I thought sadly of poor, sick Eoinín sitting on the clifftop watching them go. When they returned in the spring, I felt an aching sorrow that he was no longer there to see their return. So vivid was Eoinín to me that when I walked the fields he was beside me. I saw those same fields through the gaze of Joseph Mary Plunkett in his poem 'I See His Blood Upon the Rose'. God and Nature were inseparable in the creative vision of these men of 1916.

When we in Innishannon came to commemorate the 1916 Rising a hundred years later, an event inspired by

these poets and visionaries, it seemed right to do something that would be in harmony with their love of nature. It was decided to plant seven trees as a salutation to the seven signatories of the declaration. The trees would be planted in the village centre and given sufficient space ultimately to reach their full magnificence. The Bleach was the obvious location, edging the much-used walk over which they would in time create an avenue.

Normally it is advised to begin tree-planting with a sapling as they make better progress, but when a tree is being planted on a ceremonial occasion you need one that makes a statement. Seven trees representing the seven signatories of the Proclamation required seven big statements. So a visit to the nearby tree nursery of Nangle & Niesen was on the agenda. From them we had bought the trees for our Millennium Grove in 2000. As I am now retired, I am readily available for such outings, which is a great blessing. So, with a daughter, who happened to have a day off, and a three-year-old granddaughter, who thought that it was all a great adventure, we headed up the hill to the tree farm. On arriving there, on the week before Easter 2016, we were met by a young man I had not met before. It was Ronan Nangle, and he sure knew his trees.

We boarded his jeep and set off around the hundred-acre tree farm. Trees of all heights and ages saluted us on our tour of inspection. It was overawing, to say the least. I had come here leaning towards oak, but not quite sure if that was the correct choice, and left the place in a still more confused state of mind. There were just too many magnificent trees available! After much discussion and deliberation, the mud-died waters of confusion cleared, and the oaks still stood out. They were the right choice. They would live for hundreds of years and definitely see in the next centenary.

We got back to Ronan on the Monday before Easter and placed the order. They would be delivered on Holy Thursday. Costing a hundred euro each, they would come ball-rooted and be about twenty feet tall. He warned that they would need good, comfortable beds and rich compost. In today's world, everything is done by machinery, but in a GAA field that had suffered winter flooding, that was not an option. Luckily we had an alternative: the two Johns, two of our FÁS workers who are not afraid of hard work.

We also needed a man who knew about making beds for trees, and Jim McKeon, our retired horticulturist and one of our Tidy Towns volunteers, came on board. In glorious spring sunshine, the big dig began, and on the first day four large holes were made. The earth was stony and gravelly and could have been richer, but on the following day when the final holes were dug closer to the river, the earth became rich and loamy. We concluded that in earlier times this area of The Bleach could have been tidal, resulting in this sandy soil. Holes dug, the two Johns went to nearby stables and brought back a trailer-load of old, well-rotted horse manure. (Apparently it is not now permissible in polite society to say horse dung.)

The beds were ready for the trees, and, in the meantime, we were trying to organise the planting ceremony for Easter Monday and to get the word out. A bit like the Rising itself, it was all a bit last-minute and *trína chéile*. However, on Holy Thursday, the trees arrived – these were the main performers, and they were looking good! But how were these heavyweights going to be lifted down off the trailer and placed near their future resting place? The expertise of Ronan Nangle in shifting them was pretty impressive. With one of the lads catching them by the crown to control direction, he sank a small, solid, steel claw into the ball root and swung each tree effortlessly into position near its hole. With this simple technique the whole operation went seamlessly. The eagle had landed! All was well.

Along with the trees, Ronan had brought a silver spade. It belonged to the nursery and had been used in many ceremonial tree-planting events: in Mount Juliet by golfer Jack Nicklaus, and in other venues by Fred Couples, Christy O'Connor and Seve Ballesteros, and by Mary Robinson as President of Ireland. Innishannon 1916 was next in line!

Jim McKeon very wisely decided that we would have the trees standing in their specific beds with accompanying compost beneath and around them ready for planting. So this was done, and each tree stood tall and elegant, waiting to be dressed. We were ready for action. However, on Easter Sunday evening, a phone call from Jim announced that the first hole was now full of water which was not draining off, and so was not suitable for our fine oak. The decision was made to close up that hole and go to the other end of the row where the earth was actually much better. The trees had, in their own way, decided to move around The Bleach corner, which would give them a much more impressive location. Pearse, as we know, was into theatrical presentation! Was he in action here?

On Easter Monday morning, at 7am, Peter Fehily and Joe Walsh of the Tidy Towns committee dug a new and more dramatic location for PH Pearse.

At 3pm the troops gathered. We had sent out the news on the GAA and Tidy Towns text system, the local paper, the church newsletters and the noticeboard on the pole at the corner, and got it announced at the church services. Some, as suggested, came dressed in 1916 apparel.

It was a heart-warming ceremony, introduced by Elmarie Mawe, who gave a brief synopsis of the Rising in Irish and in English, followed by a reading by Margaret O'Sullivan of Pearse's poem 'Mise Éire', again in both languages:

Mise Éire:
Sine mé ná an Chailleach Bhéarra …

Then she read 'I See His Blood Upon the Rose':

I see his blood upon the rose
And in the stars the glory of his eyes,
His body gleams amid eternal snows,
His tears fall from the skies ...

Finally came a reading of the powerfully worded 1916 Proclamation, read by Peter Fehily to a silent, attentive gathering.

IRISHMEN AND IRISHWOMEN: In the name of God and of the dead generations from which she receives her old tradition of nationhood, Ireland, through us, summons her children to her flag and strikes for her freedom. ...

The Irish Republic is entitled to, and hereby claims, the allegiance of every Irishman and Irishwoman. The Republic guarantees religious and civil liberty, equal rights and equal opportunities to all its citizens, and declares its resolve to pursue the happiness and prosperity of the whole nation and of all its parts, cherishing all of the children of the nation equally, and oblivious of the differences carefully fostered by an alien Government, which have divided a minority from the majority in the past.

Then Jerry Larkin, accompanied by musicians Donal Murphy, Jimmy McCarthy and Tommy Kirwin, led a rousing rendering of the National Anthem. Fr Finbarr blessed the trees, and Elmarie read the well-known and beautiful poem 'Trees' by Joyce Kilmer, written by this American poet just three years before the Rising, in 1913, and reminding us all of the importance of trees.

Trees

I think that I shall never see
A poem lovely as a tree.

A tree whose hungry mouth is prest
Against the sweet earth's flowing breast;

A tree that looks at God all day,
And lifts her leafy arms to pray;

A tree that may in summer wear
A nest of robins in her hair;

Upon whose bosom snow has lain;
Who intimately lives with rain.

Poems are made by fools like me,
But only God can make a tree.

As the trees were being planted, the musicians played and led songs of the time. It was a communal planting, shared by all, and the children loved ladling in the earth with the small spades provided. Many of them will see these trees reach maturity and will remember their planting.

Further along the path from those trees is a huge stone which will hopefully tolerate the chiselling of a stonemason's hammer to imprint 1916–2016 on it. That and these trees will be there in 2116.

Chapter 21

Our Parish Chronicle

On the first Sunday in October, three of us gather around the kitchen table to lay out *Candlelight*. *Candlelight* is our annual village Christmas magazine and is a collection of writings and photographs from the people of the parish. In my earlier world, 'laying out' was the term used to describe the readying of the departed to meet their maker, but now we use it to mean the arranging of the pages of our Christmas annual in preparation for print – and for the appraising gaze of the parish.

Mary, Maureen and I have done this for over thirty years, and layout day is the fruition of a yearly round-up of contributions. Over the previous few months, we have begged, cajoled and entreated the people of the parish to put pen

to paper or to sit at their laptops. The layout of any publication varies from edition to edition, but when the subscribers encompass everyone in the parish who has agreed to come on board, the final edition can often be at total variance with the original plan. The contributors have free rein, as the object of the exercise is to act as a true parish voice, and this results in a potpourri of articles – recent, historical, fiction, non-fiction and whatever you feel like writing about. You name it, it ends up on our kitchen table. Some years we have too much and other years not enough, and we can be amazed, amused or dismayed by what finishes up in front of us.

The magazine usually runs to about forty or fifty pages, depending entirely on the material available. The original aim of *Candlelight* was to capture the social history of the parish as we felt that every old parishioner who died was taking a wealth of local knowledge with them, but over the years we have covered all kinds of everything, from match reports to funerals.

One important contributor was The Twin. He was our local chronicler of events as they happened, and until we pinned him down for *Candlelight* and every year published some of them, his poems and writings existed only in his head. When he died, many of his writings had been recorded in the magazine – they were often amusing recordings of events, but also contained dates and facts that would otherwise have been forgotten. Then sometimes the children of people who had written an article years previously would come looking for that back issue of *Candlelight* when the parent passed away. Then the article became extremely precious to them. All parish activities, including GAA games, soccer, rowing, Tidy Towns triumphs and every conceivable achievement is recorded, with accompanying photographs. There is a recurring parish joke that if you appear in *Candlelight* you are history, but in reality this is not the case because much of the material is actually current. It is important to record the present as well as the past for the future.

The real gems are the old photographs that come down out of people's attics or are resurrected when people declutter or move house. Old school photographs, in particular, arouse amazing interest. Last year, somebody unearthed a 1902 school photograph in which not even one child could be identified. Two of us went to the school, where, thankfully, they still had the old roll books stored away, and, after days of poring over them, we actually succeeded in identifying all the children. Some of the great-grandchildren of the children in that photograph are now in our school, and it was uncanny to see the likeness that a particular child in Senior Infants had to her great-grandmother of 1902. It was also lovely to find that sometimes a first name is carried down through the generations of a family, almost like an identifying branch on a family tree.

This undertaking of identifying the children in the old school photograph, though painstaking and time-consuming, was a fascinating experience. Some old black-and-white school photographs can be surprisingly clear, and the ones of the entire school group rather than of individuals are in later years far more interesting. Sometimes there might be just one copy of a group photo still existing in the parish, but when we publish it then everybody has a copy for their family archives, which is very satisfying.

When we started *Candlelight* in 1984, we had no idea where it would take us, but it has been an interesting journey. Now to browse through the early issues is to look back at a very different Innishannon: no traffic lights at the corner, no houses on The Lawn and no housing estates on the outskirts of the village. A few years ago, in order to capture this in greater detail, we did a chronicle of the way the village has changed within living memory. When houses get turned into businesses or vice versa, or two small houses are blended into one, you soon forget how the street looked previously. My own realisation of this came about when a man who had grown up here came home after some years away, and he and I walked the village, trying to recapture the way it was when he was a child. We were hard put to remember how it had been before the alterations had changed its face. So, for the following *Candlelight*, we went around to all the old residents and did a write-up and layout of the way it was. This then led

to the realisation that some of the farms around the parish had also changed hands down through the years, and only the farmers living in adjoining farms could now remember the names of the previous owners. So we are now in the throes of creating a 'within living memory' record of the townlands all around the parish. Sometimes ancient history is well documented, but the 'within living memory' history can disappear with the one who remembers.

When we published the first *Candlelight,* we didn't have a clue how to go about it and had to go around with a begging bowl to cover the costs. Then for a few years we broke even, and then we copped on and decided that it had to pay for itself – and eventually we got smart and began to make a profit. This profit, though not enormous, has been sown back into long-term projects to benefit the village. *Candlelight* money has kick-started the funding for the sculpture of Billy the Blacksmith at the western end of the village and the Horse and Rider sculpture at the eastern end. It has also restored a valuable old historic map dating back to the famine, where each house and townland in the parish is numbered with an accompanying list of occupiers along the sides. This map is now safely on display in St Mary's Church, where it can be referred to by people coming back to check their ancestral roots. We are currently collecting money to erect a sculpture of the Charter School children who have given their name to one corner of the village where their school stood in 1750. There were fifty Charter Schools all around Ireland, but these children are not commemorated anywhere.

Every year, at the front of the magazine, we put the photograph of a child holding a lighted candle to represent the Christmas season, and now we are into the second generation, with the children of the first *Candlelight* children following in their parents' footsteps. All the previous children form a frame around the current child.

The primary aim of *Candlelight* is to record the past and present story of Innishannon for future generations. It is posted all over the world to keep Innishannon people abroad in touch with their home place. The locals love it, and it is now part of our Innishannon Christmas.

Chapter 22

When They Return

There was a note on the kitchen table. Bullet message, meaningless to anyone but myself. 'Woman – America. Ellie – Nonie. July. Ring.' My son Mike is not long-winded like his mother. He always uses one word where six are needed, while I usually use six where one would suffice. I got the gist of his message, and there was a number to call.

Ellie and Nonie had been the chapel women here when I first came to the village in my early twenties. They were then in their seventies and are now, of course, long gone. Neither of them had children so this had to be a descendant of their sister who had emigrated and must have finished up in America. I had become well accustomed over my years in the village to people returning to look up their family

roots, and I knew about their hunger to find out everything they could about their ancestors. Usually they appear out of the blue and expect to be able to reach back about a hundred years in one hour. Sometimes they can be lucky and meet someone on the street who may have local knowledge, or, if not, are helpful enough to channel them in the right direction. Or they may be unlucky and meet a newcomer or passer-by who knows absolutely nothing about the place and hasn't got the faintest idea what they are talking about. Worse again, they could meet a local who has no interest in the history of the place and who hardly knows the name of his own grandmother and hasn't the slightest interest in being helpful. So this vital first encounter, whilst being a matter of pure luck, can make all the difference to people who come back in search of their roots. But this woman was taking no chances. She meant business. I was impressed. As well as that, I had fond memories of Ellie and Nonie and would be happy to help their returning descendants.

I was reared in a house where eight generations of our family had lived and where descendants of emigrants often returned, and when they did, my parents gave them the time and welcome that they felt was due to anyone who had roots in our farm. I now felt the same about anyone returning to our village. When I came here first, there were many people willing and able to do this, but in more recent years, sourcing the knowledge they are hoping for has become more difficult.

Ellie and Nonie had done a lot for our parish because, as chapel women, they had often gone above and beyond the call of duty. They washed the altar linen, did the flowers, polished the brasses, cleaned the church, trained the altar boys (sometimes the priests), kept track of funerals, christenings and weddings and knew who was buried in every corner of the graveyard. They were an encyclopedia of church knowledge as their mother and grandmother had been before them. Our parish owed the family a huge debt of gratitude. It was payback time. So I went to look at their gravestone. It was a fine stone, located behind the church and inscribed with all their family names and dates, but it could be cleaner! So Fr Finbarr decided that the parish would pay to have it cleaned up.

Before I got around to ringing the woman in America, a letter came with the day and date of her arrival. I checked my diary to make sure I was free and in Innishannon on that date. I marked the day in the calendar too. When the day arrived, I answered a knock on my door to find not one but six Americans on the doorstep. My well-organised correspondent, Patty, introduced me to her husband, her brother and his wife and two friends who had never previously been to Ireland. They were charming people. We sat around in the front room, and I read them a poem that I had written about Ellie, Patty's great-aunt. Then we walked up to the church where her great-great-grandmother and

great-aunts had spent their working lives. On the way up, we passed the location of the original family home and the site of the little shop where Ellie and Nonie had sold sweets to the children going to and coming from school. Where their little house, shop and haggard once stood are now two modern townhouses. I have often secretly wished that these houses had been called Tig Ellie and Tig Nonie.

Patty and her brother were delighted to meet and talk with someone who had known their great-aunts, whom Patty had visited with her mother when she was a child. She smiled as she recalled that she had been slightly in awe of these somewhat austere ladies who had seemed to this young American child to be from another planet. Still, she never forgot them and how much the visit had meant to her mother. Years later, when Ellie and Nonie were both dead, she and her mother had made a return visit, and Patty remembered how disappointed her mother had been when they could find nobody who remembered the aunts. 'So this time,' she told me, 'I was taking no chances.' Then I understood the reason for all her forward planning.

After tea and much talk, I invited them to come back another day when I would have rounded up some of the neighbours who, as children, might have known Ellie and Nonie. I made a few phone calls to neighbours who, unlike me had gone to school in the village, and, indeed, they had great childhood memories of Ellie and Nonie, and also of their brother, Jerry 'the Miller', who had worked in the mill across the road. There is no substitute for the knowledge of a place that those who have gone to school and grown up there have acquired. During childhood you unconsciously absorb the ambience of your own place, which, like an unread book, lies within you.

So, a few days later, some of these neighbours came for tea. We all sat around for hours, and there was great laughter and fun as stories of Ellie and Nonie and their brother Jerry were relayed. These old neighbours had an in-depth knowledge of the family. As children, they had bought sweets in Ellie and Nonie's little shop. The farmers in the group had, as young lads, brought grain to the mill and had great recall of Jerry. The locals enjoyed the tea and talk and reminiscing as much as the visitors did.

The following Saturday night, the Americans came to Mass in our church, and for Patty and her brother it was a very emotional experience of family remembrances. Their American travelling companions were in awe of the long-tailed roots of their Irish-American friends. After Mass, they met more neighbours who had known the great-aunts and great-uncle, and we again gathered around the kitchen table and did more catch-up on their family history.

Before the Americans left Innishannon, I asked Patty if she would write an article for *Candlelight*, and, as I had come to expect from her, it arrived shortly afterwards.

Chapter 23

Home Is a Community

We began this book with tea under Uncle Jacky's apple tree and then meandered through different scenes of village life. In many ways, village living is a cameo of life anywhere: it is the people who give colour and richness to it. When new people move in, they may wish to add value to the community by being part of it, or they may choose to be non-productive members and remain behind their own door. If they so decide, they will be left there, but if they come out and become part of the place where they now live they soon integrate and enrich their own life and the lives of those around them. All the improvements to our village have been achieved by people working together, the tried-and-tested *meitheal* system when we all get together and share the planning and the achieving. It enriches us as a community and makes this a good place to live.

Innishannon is blessed to be surrounded by a well-rooted, solid farming community, who come on board when there is a big job to be done. Also, we have the plus of a 'round up the usual suspects' system, and these people come with a positive 'can do' attitude. They are the lifeblood of the community. Their answer to a call asking for help on any given project is always, 'I'll be there.' They are usually busy people, but never perceive themselves as being too busy to get involved and help out. There is the old saying, of course, that if you want something done ask a busy person, and you really see the truth in that when organising voluntary labour.

Let us walk through the village and have a look at the projects that have been done by our voluntary labour. In recent years, one of our biggest projects was the Millennium Grove. As you enter the village on the road from Cork, you see on your left a grove of sixteen-year-old trees that are now beginning to mature. This grove was our Millennium statement. It had been waste ground, but we cleared it in preparation for the planting of these Millennium trees. All this work was achieved by hard-graft, voluntary labour. The trees, sponsored by local people, were ball-rooted, making them more expensive than the bare-rooted variety, but it was worth it as it got them off to a good start, which was further fortified by a bed of rich topsoil and old horse manure from nearby riding stables. A *meitheal* gathered in the dying days of the old millennium to plant the trees, and because their planting marked this special occasion, their age will always be remembered.

During the following sixteen years, we also planted three hundred trees on the opposite bank. Here again the *meitheal* system came into play, and tea and cake were brought along to introduce a softening and sociable aspect to the hard endeavour. During these gatherings, neighbours met and new residents were integrated into the community. These trees will eventually become a complete wood, requiring little maintenance, and will greatly enhance the environment by absorbing some of the harmful emissions from the endless stream of traffic passing by them into West Cork.

Closer to the village around the stone monument bearing our village name are many specimen trees commemorating special events. Here is a *Cedrus deodara*, which was bought at a gardening talk in our local pub. It spent a few years in a large pot and was then transplanted out here. It is now beginning to take off and will eventually grow into a magnificent tree. Hopefully no maniac will ever get to it with a saw! If you never plant a tree, you will happily cut one down, not realising how long it takes a tree to mature.

Providing a backdrop to all these trees is an ever-strengthening beech hedge that again was planted by a *meitheal* a few years back. In spring, this hedge comes alive in a vivid sap green, then deepens in summer into a stronger hue and turns into a gorgeous bronze in winter.

The jewel in the crown at the entrance to our village is the wonderful sculpture of the Horse and Rider at Bothairín an Átha. This symbolic sculpture of a workhorse and cloaked rider breathe the antiquity of another era. It alerts new arrivals that they are about to enter a storied and historic place, and it encapsulates the origins of our village. This river ford was where the settlement began. In ancient times, when waterways were the arteries of the country, while roads were still dirt tracks and before bridges were built, river crossings were of huge commercial importance. This river crossing was the birthplace of our village. The Bandon river is tidal up to this point, and when the tide withdrew down to Kinsale harbour, the river was fordable. The village grew up around that ford. Seven years ago, we erected the sculpture to commemorate our ancestors and to mark the gateway – by horse – into the village and West Cork. This approach road is kept in pristine condition by Jim and Antoinette, who live here and regularly do the hard job of picking litter. The litter-pickers who live along the approach roads into the village are a vital link in the chain of our village maintenance.

Then you come to the row of little houses formerly the property of the Frewen estate, who were once landlords here, and beside them is the grotto, a green haven where a young weeping willow, planted in 2005, is now catching up with an older companion willow, planted thirty years earlier by the Tidy Towns committee. A *meitheal* gathers here every summer to give the grotto an overhaul and afterwards enjoy a cup of tea and chat. Under the spout of a red pump on the pathway outside the grotto we have recently placed an old water trough. This was originally the iron trough for watering the priest's horse in the presbytery. That need is long gone, and the old trough has now become a flower container. Across the road, the old Barrack Well, from which the villagers formerly drew their water, has been restored, and beside it is a fine barracks, now, happily, the home of our new young guard and his family.

The beautiful and historic Market House, the only one of its kind in Ireland, catches your eye as you round the village corner. Facing you then is the Adderley Lawn Wall of the original Innishannon House. The first landlord, Thomas Adderley, built his family home beside Bothairín an Átha, and for security reasons – and to prevent the natives polluting his view – surrounded himself with a high wall. The arched wall still remains today and is one of the features of our village.

In front of this is sited a bright red cart, laden with flowers and surrounded by overflowing barrels in similar profusion, watered and cared for by Willie. This brilliant display is continued in the planted troughs in front of the old ivied

Innishannon Lawn Wall whose arches are draped with hanging baskets, watered and cared for by Catherine and Phil, who live behind the arches. Along the main street and on the hill up to St Mary's Church, many houses and businesses put out window boxes and hanging baskets every year. The hope is that some year every house will have a window box!

As you go through the village, you will see many black and red plaques on the walls. If you are on a walkabout, you can read these plaques, which tell the interesting history of the village buildings.

As you approach the western end of the village, to your right is an old stone wall, and in 1750 behind this wall stood a Charter School. These schools, of which there were fifty around Ireland, were the precursors of the national school system. This crossroads was originally known as Charter School Cross. Beside this wall, a flower-laden scarlet wheelbarrow, rescued in a battered state from a ditch outside the village, has been given a new lease of life. Finally, over the bridge and facing you, in front of the restored forge, is the sculpture of Billy the Blacksmith. This sculpture is a well-known landmark on the road to West Cork. Here in this forge Billy's family plied their trade for generations. On the corner opposite Billy is a large boat overflowing with flowers and behind it a little walled slope to the river traditionally known as The Hatchery, the brainchild of the entrepreneurial landlord Mortimer Frewen.

As you round the last corner out of Innishannon, your final sighting is of Billy the Blacksmith with his hammer raised in farewell. Our Horse receives you into the village, and our Blacksmith bids you farewell as you leave! They are the guardians at each end of our village.

The winds of change have blown through our village, but by blending our historical past with these changes we enrich our home place and preserve it for the future. The *meitheal* system of togetherness strengthens our sense of community – because as well as working together we always take the time to have tea and talk.